Simple Dash Diet Cookbook for Beginners

The Ultimate Dash Diet Book with Low Sodium
Recipes to Lower Your Blood Pressure.

Includes a 30-Day Dash Diet Meal Plan.

Phyllis Fletcher

Table of Contents

# Introduction

Do you want to find a permanent solution to your high blood pressure? Have you had trouble finding a heart-healthy diet that you can stick to and include in your daily life? If this describes you, know that you're not alone. Hypertension, or high blood pressure, affects millions of individuals worldwide and can have severe consequences if not treated properly. The good news is that you've come to the right place because this book is formatted to help you deal with this issue head-on.

Introducing "Simple Dash Diet Cookbook for Beginners: The Ultimate Dash Diet Book with Low Sodium Recipes to Lower Your Blood Pressure." This in-depth manual provides an easy and tasty way to lower blood pressure and boost health. According to scientists, the DASH (Dietary Approaches to Stop Hypertension) Diet is one of the most effective approaches to reducing blood pressure and improving heart health. The DASH Diet encourages you to improve your health by limiting unhealthy foods and increasing those that are good for you.

In this book, we provide you with a wide variety of delicious dishes that adhere to DASH Diet principles so that you never have to choose between nourishing your health and satisfying your taste buds. Each recipe, from filling breakfasts and satisfying lunches to delicious dinners and desserts, has been carefully developed to give you the right flavor and nutrition.

Let me start by telling you a little about myself as the author of this book and why you should trust me to help you improve your health. I'm Phyllis Fletcher, a certified nutritionist who has helped many people combat obesity, diabetes, heart disease, hypertension, and hypertension during my career. I attended Texas Women's University for my Bachelor's and Master's degrees in nutrition because I am deeply interested in the subject and its potential for improving people's health.

I've collaborated with chefs and food experts to develop tasty and nutritious meal plans. Seeing my clients' lives and health improve due to my work is incredibly rewarding. This book aims to equip you with the knowledge, skills, and enthusiasm I have for healthy cooking to help you take care of your health.

Your blood pressure will drop, and you'll get many other health benefits when you follow the DASH Diet plan outlined in this cookbook. If you embrace a lifestyle centered on fueling your body with wholesome foods, you can look forward to more energy, improved mental clarity, and easier weight management. The DASH Diet isn't simply a quick fix; it's a long-term strategy for health that can set you on the path to greater vitality.

Many people who have adopted the DASH diet attest to its efficacy and have seen dramatic changes in their health. Testimonials from people whose lives have been changed by following this book's meal plans and dishes will motivate and encourage you.

I have complete faith that the "Simple Dash Diet Cookbook for Beginners" will be invaluable as you work to improve your health. You can significantly lower your blood pressure and improve your health by making these delicious and healthy meals a regular diet.

Putting off caring for your health might have devastating results. High blood pressure can lead to heart disease, stroke, and other serious health problems when left untreated. Adopting the DASH Diet today will allow you to take charge of your health and stave off potential difficulties in the future.

In "Simple Dash Diet Cookbook for Beginners," you will find a wealth of information that will change how you think about food and how you feel. Let's start improving our health and well-being one tasty recipe at a time. Let's begin this life-changing journey today and find the key to a better, healthier self.

Let's turn the page and begin our journey to improved health through the kitchen!

Chapter 1
The DASH Diet:
What You Need to Know

When it comes to improving heart health and reducing blood pressure, the DASH (Dietary Approaches to Stop Hypertension) Diet is no fleeting trend. The DASH Diet encourages you to take charge of your health by considering which foods you eat and why. Here, we'll break down the DASH Diet's main tenets and see how they can improve your health in the long run.

A Breakdown of the Various Food Categories

To get the health benefits promised by the DASH Diet, eating a variety of foods high in vitamins, minerals, and other beneficial substances is important. These categories of diet consist of:

The best fruits to eat are those that are either fresh, frozen, or canned without any added sugars. They're naturally sweet, packed with vitamins and fiber, and will satisfy your sweet tooth.

Colorful, varied vegetables should make up a large amount of your plate. They are a great addition to your diet because of their low-calorie count and rich vitamin, mineral, and antioxidant content.

Go for whole grains like brown rice, quinoa, oats, and whole wheat bread instead of refined grains. The high fiber content of whole grains promotes healthy digestion and steady blood sugar.

Lean Proteins: Go for fish, chicken, beans, lentils, and tofu as lean protein options. These proteins supply essential nutrients without the high levels of saturated fat often found in animal products.

Calcium and other critical elements can be supplied to your body by consuming low-fat or fat-free dairy products or non-dairy alternatives like almond or soy milk.

The Recommended Daily Caloric Intake and Serving Sizes

The success of the DASH Diet hinges on your ability to estimate serving amounts properly. Depending on factors like age, gender, and degree of activity, the number of servings per food group you should aim for each day can change. Included in a daily 2,000-calorie eating plan are the following:

- Six to eight portions of cereal
- 4–5 veggie servings per day
- 4–5 fruit servings per day
- 2–3 dairy or dairy-alternative servings per day
- Consume no more than 2 servings of meat, fish, or poultry per week.
- Eat 4–5 ounces of legumes, nuts, and seeds weekly.

Sodium and Potassium

Both potassium and sodium are essential in maintaining healthy blood pressure. The abundance of potassium in the DASH Diet mitigates some of the adverse effects of sodium. To maintain normal blood pressure, it is recommended to consume more potassium and less sodium. Bananas, oranges, potatoes, spinach, and beans are all good sources of potassium.

The Most Effective Methods for Reducing Unhealthy Fats

The DASH Diet emphasizes cutting back on saturated and trans fats, which contribute to elevated cholesterol and an increased risk of heart disease. To reduce intake of bad fats:

Opt for leaner cuts and trim any excess fat when preparing meat.

Swap out butter and hydrogenated oils for olive oil and other heart-healthy oils.

Avoid eating too many fatty, processed, or fried meals.

To better support your heart health, decrease your blood pressure, and enjoy a well-balanced, nutritious diet that supports your overall health, it is important to understand and practice the key concepts of the DASH Diet. Let's continue to the following part, exploring many tasty recipes that adhere to the DASH Diet guidelines.

Chapter 2
The DASH Diet's Approved and Prohibited Foods

The DASH Diet is effective because it prioritizes heart-healthy and nutrient-dense foods while reducing the intake of items linked to hypertension and other health problems. In this section, we will discuss the DASH Diet's preferred and permitted foods and those that should be avoided or consumed in moderation.

DASH Diet-Approved Foods

Fruits and veggies abound, so load up your platter with as many colors as possible. These vitamin, mineral, and antioxidant-rich meals are great for your heart and your health in general.

Brown rice, quinoa, oats, and whole wheat are all examples of whole grains that are preferable to refined grains. Because of their high fiber and vitamin content, whole grains might keep you feeling full for longer.

Eat lean proteins like skinless chicken and fish and beans, lentils, and tofu. These alternatives have fewer unhealthy saturated fats and are better for your heart.

Reduce the amount of fat in your diet by consuming low-fat or fat-free dairy products such as milk, yogurt, and cheese. Almond, soy, and oat milk, without added sugar, are good alternatives to cow's milk if you're lactose intolerant.

Eat a wide range of nuts, seeds, and legumes, but keep portions in check. They contain beneficial nutrients like fiber, protein, and healthy fats that may aid in controlling blood sugar and protecting the cardiovascular system.

Foods to Avoid or Consume in Moderation When On the DASH Diet

Limit your consumption of high-sodium foods, as doing so can help lower blood pressure. Limit your intake of processed foods, canned soups, salty snacks, and fast food because of their high sodium content.

Sweets and Added Sugars: The DASH Diet does not call for total abstinence from sweets, although moderation is key. Cut back on sodas, sweets, and desserts as much as possible.

Reduce fatty meats, butter, and baked goods made with hydrogenated oils because they are high in saturated and trans fats. These fats elevate LDL cholesterol and, therefore, the risk of heart disease.

While drinking alcohol in moderation may have some benefits, heavy drinking harms health. If you decide to drink, do it responsibly and within the limits recommended by your doctor.

Finding a Happy Medium

Remember that the DASH Diet is not about restriction but about developing a healthy, long-term relationship with food. While it's true that you should cut back on a few things, you deserve a treat every once in a while. The trick is to consume mostly healthy things and reward yourself sometimes.

Meal Preparation and Planning

Plan and prepare your meals ahead of time to ease into the DASH Diet. This will help you stick to the DASH Diet guidelines and avoid reaching for unhealthy fast food when time is of the essence.

You can improve your heart, blood pressure, and overall health by sticking to the DASH Diet's list of approved and disapproved items. The next chapter will explore recipes that highlight the delightful potential of the DASH Diet. Prepare to embark on a tasty path to improved health!

Chapter 3
30-Day Meal Plan

DAY	BREAKFAST	LUNCH	DINNER	SNACK
1	Spinach and Feta Omelet	Mediterranean Chickpea Salad	Lemon Herb Baked Salmon	Cucumber Dill Yogurt Bites
2	Lemon Chia Seed Muffins	Turkey and Quinoa Stuffed Zucchini Boats	Quinoa-Stuffed Bell Peppers	Kale Chips with Sea Salt
3	Breakfast Stuffed Sweet Potatoes	Lemon Garlic Shrimp and Asparagus Stir Fry	Moroccan Chickpea Stew	Mexican Cauliflower Rice
4	Zucchini and Mushroom Frittata	Grilled Lemon Herb Chicken	Garlic Shrimp and Broccoli Stir-fry	Baked Sweet Potato Fries
5	Orange-Cranberry Quinoa Porridge	Veggie Fajita Lettuce Wraps	Greek Chicken Souvlaki Skewers	Roasted Garlic Brussels Sprouts
6	Banana Nut Overnight Oats	Baked Cod with Herbed Quinoa	Vegetable Lentil Curry	Herb-Roasted Turnip Wedges
7	Tomato and Basil Egg White Scramble	Greek Yogurt Chicken Salad Lettuce Wraps	Balsamic Glazed Chicken Thighs	Mango Avocado Salsa
8	Pineapple Coconut Chia Pudding	Cauliflower Rice and Black Bean Burrito Bowl	Asian Turkey Lettuce Wraps	Greek Yogurt Cucumber Dip
9	Greek Yogurt Parfait with Berries and Almonds	Teriyaki Tofu and Veggie Skewers	Lemon Garlic Roasted Chicken	Spicy Edamame
10	Breakfast Burrito with Black Beans and Avocado	Spaghetti Squash with Turkey Bolognese	Spicy Cajun Shrimp and Quinoa	Zucchini Noodle Salad with Lemon Dressing

11	Cheddar and Broccoli Egg Muffins	Quinoa and Roasted Vegetable Buddha Bowl	Grilled Portobello Mushroom Steaks	Caprese Skewers with Balsamic Glaze
12	Roasted Vegetable Breakfast Hash	Cilantro Lime Shrimp Tacos	Blackened Tilapia with Mango Salsa	Eggplant and Tomato Stacks
13	Almond Butter Banana Toast	Baked Chicken and Sweet Potato Fries	Mexican Cauliflower Rice Bowl	Smoked Salmon Cucumber Bites
14	Chocolate Protein Pancakes	Tomato Basil Quinoa Salad	Herb-Marinated Grilled Pork Tenderloin	Quinoa Tabbouleh
15	Quinoa and Black Bean Breakfast Bowl	Turkey Meatball Lettuce Wraps	Mediterranean Zucchini Noodles with Shrimp	Baked Parmesan Zucchini Rounds
16	Lemon Poppy Seed Muffins	Eggplant and Chickpea Curry	Thai Coconut Curry Chicken	Lemon Herb Asparagus Spears
17	Cottage Cheese and Berry Bowl	Garlic Shrimp and Spinach Salad	Stuffed Bell Peppers with Turkey and Quinoa	Mango Avocado Salsa
18	Baked Egg Avocado Boats	Lemon Dill Salmon with Steamed Broccoli	Pesto Zucchini Noodles with Grilled Chicken	Cucumber Dill Yogurt Bites
19	Pomegranate and Pistachio Yogurt Parfait	Black Bean and Avocado Wrap	Lemon Herb Grilled Turkey Burgers	Lemon Herb Asparagus Spears
20	Cinnamon Raisin French Toast	Lemon Herb Grilled Turkey Burgers	Lemon Herb Baked Salmon	Cucumber Dill Yogurt Bites
21	Lemon Chia Seed Muffins	Grilled Lemon Herb Chicken	Garlic Shrimp and Broccoli Stir-fry	Kale Chips with Sea Salt
22	Breakfast Stuffed Sweet Potatoes	Lemon Garlic Shrimp and Asparagus Stir Fry	Moroccan Chickpea Stew	Mexican Cauliflower Rice

23	Zucchini and Mushroom Frittata	Turkey and Quinoa Stuffed Zucchini Boats	Quinoa-Stuffed Bell Peppers	Baked Sweet Potato Fries
24	Orange-Cranberry Quinoa Porridge	Veggie Fajita Lettuce Wraps	Greek Chicken Souvlaki Skewers	Roasted Garlic Brussels Sprouts
25	Banana Nut Overnight Oats	Baked Cod with Herbed Quinoa	Vegetable Lentil Curry	Herb-Roasted Turnip Wedges
26	Tomato and Basil Egg White Scramble	Greek Yogurt Chicken Salad Lettuce Wraps	Balsamic Glazed Chicken Thighs	Mango Avocado Salsa
27	Pineapple Coconut Chia Pudding	Cauliflower Rice and Black Bean Burrito Bowl	Asian Turkey Lettuce Wraps	Greek Yogurt Cucumber Dip
28	Greek Yogurt Parfait with Berries and Almonds	Teriyaki Tofu and Veggie Skewers	Lemon Garlic Roasted Chicken	Spicy Edamame
29	Breakfast Burrito with Black Beans and Avocado	Spaghetti Squash with Turkey Bolognese	Spicy Cajun Shrimp and Quinoa	Zucchini Noodle Salad with Lemon Dressing
30	Cheddar and Broccoli Egg Muffins	Quinoa and Roasted Vegetable Buddha Bowl	Grilled Portobello Mushroom Steaks	Caprese Skewers with Balsamic Glaze

Breakfast Recipes

Spinach and Feta Omelet

🍳 *Prep time: 10 minutes*

🍲 *Cook time: 10 minutes*

🍽 *Servings: 2*

🍵 **Ingredients:**

- 4 large eggs
- 1 cup fresh spinach, chopped
- 1/4 cup feta cheese crumbles
- 1/4 cup diced tomatoes
- 1/4 cup diced red bell pepper
- 1/4 teaspoon dried oregano
- 1/4 teaspoon black pepper
- 1/8 teaspoon salt (optional)
- 1 teaspoon olive oil

▧ **Directions:**

1. In a medium bowl, whisk the eggs until fully beaten. Add the feta cheese, diced tomatoes, red bell pepper, and eggs to the chopped spinach.
2. Add the dried oregano, black pepper, and salt (if using) to the egg mixture. Mix everything thoroughly.
3. Heat a nonstick skillet to medium-high. Pour the olive oil into the pan, then swirl to coat everything.
4. Spread the egg mixture evenly in the skillet after pouring in half of it.
5. Cook the omelet for about 2-3 minutes or until the bottom is set and lightly browned.
6. Carefully flip the omelet using a spatula and cook the other side for another 2-3 minutes, or until it is fully cooked through.
7. To make a second omelet, use the leftover egg mixture and transfer the cooked omelet to a plate.
8. Serve the Spinach and Feta Omelets hot and enjoy a delicious and nutritious Dash diet-approved breakfast!

Nutritional Info Per Serving:

Calories: 210 | Fats: 14g | Carbs: 5g | Proteins: 16g | Potassium: 356mg | Sodium: 370mg

Lemon Chia Seed Muffins

🍳 *Prep time: 15 minutes*

🍲 *Cook time: 20 minutes*

🍽 *Servings: 12 muffins*

🍵 **Ingredients:**

- 1 1/2 cups whole wheat flour
- 1/2 cup almond flour
- 1/2 cup chia seeds
- 1 teaspoon baking powder
- 1/2 teaspoon baking soda
- 1/4 teaspoon salt
- 2 large eggs
- 1/2 cup honey (or maple syrup as a vegan alternative)
- 1/4 cup olive oil
- 1 cup unsweetened almond milk (or other milk of your choice)
- Zest of 2 lemons
- Juice of 1 lemon
- 1 teaspoon vanilla extract

▧ **Directions:**

1. Line a muffin tray with paper liners or lightly grease it and preheat your oven to 350°F (175°C).
2. In a big mixing bowl, combine the whole wheat flour, almond flour, chia seeds, baking powder, baking soda, and salt.
3. Beat the eggs in a different bowl; add the honey (or maple syrup), olive oil, unsweetened almond milk, lemon juice, lemon zest, and vanilla extract afterward.
4. Mix the dry ingredients briefly after adding the liquid components. Avoid overmixing; some lumps are acceptable.

5. Fill each muffin cup about three-quarters, then divide the batter among them evenly.
6. Bake for 18 to 20 minutes in a preheated oven, or until a toothpick inserted in the center of a muffin comes out clean
7. After removing the muffins from the oven, allow them to cool in the pan for a short while before moving them to a wire rack to finish cooling.
8. Your Lemon Chia Seed Muffins are ready to be enjoyed as a delectable and healthy breakfast or snack after they have cooled.

Nutritional Info Per Serving
(1 muffin):

Calories: 190 | Fats: 9g | Carbs: 25g | Proteins: 5g | Potassium: 130mg | Sodium: 120mg

Stuffed Breakfast Sweet Potatoes

Prep time: 10 minutes

Cook time: 40 minutes

Servings: 2

Ingredients:

- 2 medium sweet potatoes
- 4 large eggs
- 1 cup baby spinach, chopped
- 1/2 cup diced red bell pepper
- 1/4 cup diced onion
- 1/4 cup shredded cheddar cheese
- 2 tablespoons olive oil
- 1/2 teaspoon paprika
- Salt and pepper to taste

Directions:

1. Set the oven temperature to 400°F (200°C).
2. Wash the sweet potatoes and poke them several times with a fork. Bake them for 35 to 40 minutes in a preheated oven, or until a knife inserted into them comes out clean.
3. While the sweet potatoes are roasting, heat one tablespoon of olive oil in a skillet over medium heat. Add the red bell pepper and diced onion and cook for three to four minutes, or until they are soft and just starting to caramelize.
4. After 2 minutes of heating in the skillet with the chopped spinach, the baby spinach will wilt. Add salt, pepper, and paprika to taste after stirring everything together.
5. Create a small well in the center of the vegetable mixture in the skillet and crack one egg into it. Repeat with the other three eggs, distributing them evenly in the skillet.
6. Place a lid on the skillet and reduce the heat to low. Cook the eggs for about 4-5 minutes, or until the whites are set but the yolks are still relatively runny.
7. Once the sweet potatoes are done baking, let them cool slightly, then slice them in half lengthwise.
8. Gently scoop out some of the flesh from each sweet potato half, creating a cavity for the filling.
9. Divide the vegetable and egg mixture equally among the sweet potato halves, filling them generously.
10. Sprinkle shredded cheddar cheese over each stuffed sweet potato.
11. Place the stuffed sweet potatoes back in the oven for about 2-3 minutes or until the cheese is melted and bubbly.
12. After taking the stuffed sweet potatoes out of the oven, add the final tablespoon of olive oil.
13. Serve the Stuffed Breakfast Sweet Potatoes while they are still warm, and enjoy a delicious, nutrient-packed breakfast to kickstart your day!

Zucchini and Mushroom Frittata

🍴 *Prep time: 15 minutes*

🍲 *Cook time: 25 minutes*

🍽 *Servings: 4*

🥄 **Ingredients:**

- 6 large eggs
- 1 medium zucchini, sliced into rounds
- 1 cup sliced mushrooms (button mushrooms or any variety you prefer)
- 1/2 cup diced red bell pepper
- 1/4 cup diced onion
- 1/4 cup grated Parmesan cheese
- 2 tablespoons olive oil
- 2 tablespoons chopped fresh parsley
- 1/2 teaspoon dried thyme
- Salt and pepper to taste

🍳 **Directions:**

1. Set your oven to 375°F (190°C).
2. Whisk the eggs in a large mixing bowl until they are well beaten. Add salt, pepper, dried thyme, chopped parsley, and grated Parmesan cheese after stirring. Set aside the egg mixture.
3. In an oven-safe skillet (a non-stick skillet works well), heat one tablespoon of olive oil over medium heat.
4. Add the diced red bell pepper and onion to the skillet and heat for 2 to 3 minutes, or until they start to soften.
5. After adding the mushroom slices, continue to sauté for an additional 3 to 4 minutes, or until the mushrooms are cooked and just beginning to brown. Take the vegetables out of the skillet and put them aside.
6. Increase the amount of oil in the skillet by one more tablespoon. Add the zucchini slices and sauté them for 2 minutes on each side, or until they just start to turn brown. Remove the zucchini slices from the griddle and set them aside.
7. Spread the remaining zucchini slices evenly in the skillet. Pour the sautéed mushroom, red bell pepper, and onion mixture over the zucchini.
8. Give the egg mixture one final whisk and then pour it evenly over the vegetables in the skillet. Arrange the reserved zucchini slices on top.
9. Cook the frittata on the stovetop for 3 to 4 minutes at medium heat, or until the edges begin to set.
10. Bake the frittata in the preheated oven for 12 to 15 minutes, or until the eggs are completely set in the center.
11. Once the frittata is done baking, remove it from the oven (be cautious as the handle will be hot), and let it cool slightly before slicing.
12. Serve the Zucchini and Mushroom Frittata warm, and enjoy a nutritious and flavorful breakfast or brunch!

Orange-Cranberry Quinoa Porridge

🍴 *Prep time: 5 minutes*

🍲 *Cook time: 20 minutes*

🍽 *Servings: 2*

🥄 **Ingredients:**

- 1/2 cup quinoa, rinsed

- 1 cup water
- 1 cup unsweetened orange juice
- 1/2 cup dried cranberries
- 1 tablespoon honey or maple syrup (as a vegan alternative)
- 1/2 teaspoon vanilla extract
- 1/4 teaspoon ground cinnamon
- Pinch of salt
- 1/4 cup chopped nuts (e.g., almonds, walnuts, or pecans)
- 1 tablespoon chia seeds (optional)
- Greek yogurt or coconut yogurt (as a vegan alternative), for serving

⌧ Directions:

1. Combine the rinsed quinoa, water, and orange juice in a medium pot. Over high heat, bring the mixture to a boil.
2. Simmer the quinoa for about 15 minutes, or until all the liquid is absorbed and the quinoa is cooked, on low heat with the lid on the pan.
3. Place the dried cranberries in a small bowl and slightly rehydrate them with warm water while the quinoa is cooking.
4. Using a fork, fluff the cooked quinoa before adding the honey, maple syrup, vanilla essence, ground cinnamon, and a dash of salt. Drain the cranberries before adding them to the quinoa.
5. If you prefer a thicker consistency, let the porridge simmer for an additional 2-3 minutes, stirring occasionally.
6. Remove the saucepan from the heat and let the porridge cool slightly before serving.
7. Divide the Orange-Cranberry Quinoa Porridge into serving bowls. Top each bowl with chopped nuts and chia seeds (if using).
8. To add extra creaminess and nutritional value, top the porridge with a dollop of Greek yogurt or coconut yogurt.

9. Enjoy this comforting and nutritious Orange-Cranberry Quinoa Porridge as a delightful breakfast to start your day off right!

Nutritional Info Per Serving:

Calories: 340 | Fats: 8g | Carbs: 63g | Proteins: 9g | Potassium: 472mg | Sodium: 5mg

Banana Nut Overnight Oats

✂ *Prep time: 10 minutes (plus overnight chilling)*

🍲 *Cook time: 0 minutes*

🍽 *Servings: 2*

🥄 Ingredients:

- 1 cup old-fashioned rolled oats
- 1 1/2 cups unsweetened almond milk (or any milk of your choice)
- 1 ripe banana, mashed
- 2 tablespoons chopped walnuts or pecans
- 1 tablespoon honey or maple syrup (as a vegan alternative)
- 1/2 teaspoon ground cinnamon
- 1/2 teaspoon vanilla extract
- Pinch of salt
- Optional toppings:
- Sliced bananas
- Additional chopped nuts
- Drizzle of honey or maple syrup

⌧ Directions:

1. Rolled oats, almond milk, mashed banana, chopped walnuts or pecans, honey or maple syrup, ground cinnamon, vanilla essence, and a dash of salt should all be combined in a mixing bowl. Everything should be thoroughly mixed together.
2. Divide the mixture into two 8-ounce mason jars or any airtight containers with lids.

3. Refrigerate the jars or containers overnight or for at least 4-6 hours after securing the lids. Overnight, the oats will absorb the liquid and become softer.
4. The next morning, give the overnight oats a good stir to ensure everything is mixed well.
5. If desired, top the Banana Nut Overnight Oats with sliced bananas, additional chopped nuts, and a drizzle of honey or maple syrup for added sweetness.
6. Serve the delicious and creamy Banana Nut Overnight Oats straight from the jar or container, or transfer them to serving bowls.
7. Enjoy this easy and nutritious breakfast that you can prepare ahead of time for a hassle-free start to your day!

Nutritional Info Per Serving:

Calories: 320 | Fats: 11g | Carbs: 50g | Proteins: 8g | Potassium: 415mg | Sodium: 160mg

Tomato and Basil Egg White Scramble

✂ *Prep time: 5 minutes*

🍲 *Cook time: 10 minutes*

🍽 *Servings: 2*

🍳 **Ingredients:**

- 4 large egg whites
- 1 medium tomato, diced
- 2 tablespoons chopped fresh basil
- 1/4 cup diced onion
- 1/4 cup diced red bell pepper
- 1 teaspoon olive oil
- Salt and pepper to taste
- 2 tablespoons shredded mozzarella cheese (optional)

🗒 **Directions:**

1. Whip the egg whites until foamy in a bowl. Set aside after adding a dash of salt and pepper to taste.

2. Warm the olive oil in a nonstick skillet over medium heat.
3. Add the diced red bell pepper and onion to the skillet, and sauté for 2 to 3 minutes, or until they begin to soften.
4. Add the diced tomato to the skillet once the tomato has begun to soften. Continue to simmer for an additional one to two minutes.
5. Reduce the heat to low and pour the whisked egg whites over the sautéed vegetables in the skillet.
6. Gently scramble the egg whites and vegetables together using a spatula, cooking until the eggs are set but still moist and slightly creamy.
7. Stir in the chopped fresh basil, combining it well with the egg white mixture.
8. If desired, sprinkle shredded mozzarella cheese over the egg white scramble, allowing it to melt slightly.
9. When the eggs are cooked to the appropriate doneness, turn off the heat.
10. Serve the Tomato and Basil Egg White Scramble immediately while it's warm, and enjoy a light, flavorful, and protein-packed breakfast!

Nutritional Info Per Serving:

Calories: 90 | Fats: 3g | Carbs: 6g | Proteins: 10g | Potassium: 310mg | Sodium: 120mg

Pineapple Coconut Chia Pudding

✂ *Prep time: 5 minutes (plus chilling time)*

🍲 *Cook time: 0 minutes*

🍽 *Servings: 2*

🍳 **Ingredients:**

- 1 cup coconut milk (canned or carton)
- 1/4 cup chia seeds

- 1/2 cup diced fresh pineapple
- 1 tablespoon honey or maple syrup (as a vegan alternative)
- 1/4 teaspoon vanilla extract
- Pinch of salt
- Unsweetened shredded coconut, for garnish

⌧ Directions:

1. Coconut milk, chia seeds, honey or maple syrup, vanilla essence, and a dash of salt should all be combined in a bowl. To make sure the chia seeds are dispersed equally, stir thoroughly.
2. Add the diced fresh pineapple to the mixture and stir to combine.
3. Put plastic wrap over the bowl or divide the mixture into two 8-ounce mason jars or other airtight containers with lids.
4. The Pineapple Coconut Chia Pudding should be chilled in the refrigerator for at least two hours and ideally overnight. Chia seeds will thicken the mixture by absorbing liquid, giving it a pudding-like consistency.
5. Before serving, give the pudding a good stir to make sure the ingredients are well incorporated.
6. If desired, sprinkle some unsweetened shredded coconut on top for added texture and flavor.
7. Serve the Pineapple Coconut Chia Pudding chilled, and savor the delightful tropical flavors of this nutritious and satisfying breakfast or dessert!

Nutritional Info Per Serving:

Calories: 220 | Fats: 15g | Carbs: 17g | Proteins: 4g | Potassium: 215mg | Sodium: 40mg

Greek Yogurt Parfait with Berries and Almonds

⅞ Prep time: 10 minutes

☺ Cook time: 0 minutes

🍽 Servings: 2

Ingredients:

- 1 cup Greek yogurt (plain or vanilla flavored)
- 1 cup mixed berries (e.g., strawberries, blueberries, raspberries)
- 1/4 cup sliced almonds
- 1 tablespoon honey or maple syrup (optional, for added sweetness)
- 1/2 teaspoon vanilla extract
- Optional toppings:
- Fresh mint leaves as a garnish

⌧ Directions:

1. In a small bowl, combine Greek yogurt, honey, maple syrup, and vanilla extract. The flavors should be well combined.
2. Wash the mixed berries and pat them dry with a paper towel. If the strawberries are large, you can slice them into smaller pieces.
3. In two serving glasses or parfait cups, alternate layers of Greek yogurt, mixed berries, and sliced almonds.
4. Continue layering until all the ingredients are used, finishing with a layer of berries and a sprinkle of sliced almonds on top.
5. If more sweetness is wanted, drizzle a bit more honey or maple syrup on top.
6. Garnish the Greek Yogurt Parfait with Berries and Almonds with fresh mint leaves for a burst of color and aroma.
7. Serve the parfait immediately or refrigerate it for a little while before serving.
8. Enjoy this delightful and nutrient-rich Greek Yogurt Parfait as a

refreshing and satisfying breakfast or dessert!

Breakfast Burrito with Black Beans and Avocado

✂ Prep time: 15 minutes

🍲 Cook time: 10 minutes

🍽 Servings: 2

🍳 Ingredients:

- 4 large eggs
- 1 tablespoon milk
- 1/2 cup canned black beans, drained and rinsed
- 1/2 avocado, sliced
- 1/4 cup diced red bell pepper
- 2 tablespoons diced red onion
- 1/2 cup shredded cheddar cheese
- 2 whole wheat or spinach tortillas (10-inch diameter)
- 1 tablespoon olive oil
- Salt and pepper to taste
- Fresh cilantro, for garnish (optional)
- Salsa or hot sauce, for serving (optional)

✂ Directions:

1. In a bowl, thoroughly mix the eggs with the milk, salt, and pepper.
2. Heat half of the olive oil over medium heat in a non-stick skillet. Add the diced red bell pepper and red onion to the skillet, and sauté for about 2-3 minutes until they start to soften.
3. Pour the whisked eggs over the sautéed vegetables in the skillet. When the eggs are scrambled and cooked to the appropriate doneness, heat them while occasionally stirring.
4. While the eggs are cooking, warm the black beans in a small saucepan or in the microwave.
5. Once the eggs are cooked, set them aside, and wipe the skillet clean.
6. Place one tortilla on the skillet and warm it over medium heat for about 30 seconds on each side until it becomes pliable.
7. Lay the warmed tortilla flat on a plate. On the lower third of the tortilla, add half of the scrambled eggs, followed by half of the warmed black beans, sliced avocado, and shredded cheddar cheese.
8. Fold the sides of the tortilla inward and then roll it up tightly from the bottom to form a burrito.
9. Repeat steps 6 to 8 to make the second Breakfast Burrito with Black Beans and Avocado.
10. Optional: For a warm and crispy burrito, place the rolled burritos back on the skillet and cook for 1-2 minutes on each side until lightly toasted.
11. Garnish the burritos with fresh cilantro (if using).
12. Serve the Breakfast Burrito with Black Beans and Avocado with salsa or hot sauce on the side for added flavor and spice.
13. Enjoy this delicious and nutritious breakfast that's packed with protein, fiber, and healthy fats to fuel your day!

Cheddar and Broccoli Egg Muffins

✂ Prep time: 10 minutes

🍲 Cook time: 20 minutes

🍽 Servings: 6 muffins

Ingredients:

- 6 large eggs
- 1 cup chopped broccoli florets
- 1/2 cup shredded cheddar cheese
- 1/4 cup diced red bell pepper
- 1/4 cup diced onion
- 1/4 cup milk (any type you prefer)
- 1 tablespoon olive oil
- 1/2 teaspoon dried oregano
- 1/4 teaspoon garlic powder
- Salt and pepper to taste

Directions:

1. Your oven should be set to 375°F (190°C). Grease a muffin pan with cooking spray, or use paper liners.
2. In a medium dish, combine the eggs well with the milk, salt, pepper, dried oregano, and garlic powder.
3. Warm the olive oil in a pan set over medium heat. Sauté diced red bell pepper and onion for two to three minutes until they begin to soften.
4. Add the chopped broccoli florets to the skillet and continue to sauté for an additional 2 minutes until the broccoli is slightly tender.
5. Divide the sautéed vegetables evenly among the muffin cups in the tin.
6. After placing the vegetables in each muffin cup, top them with the egg mixture, filling each cup to about two-thirds.
7. Top each muffin cup with shredded cheddar cheese.
8. Bake the Cheddar and Broccoli Egg Muffins for 15-20 minutes, or until the tops are lightly browned and the eggs are set, in the preheated oven.
9. Once the muffins are done baking, remove the tin from the oven and let them cool slightly.
10. The egg muffins should be removed from the pan with care, then placed on a wire rack to complete cooling.
11. Serve the Cheddar and Broccoli Egg Muffins warm or at room temperature, and enjoy a delicious and nutritious breakfast or snack on-the-go!

Nutritional Info Per Serving (1 muffin):

Calories: 120 | Fats: 8g | Carbs: 4g | Proteins: 8g | Potassium: 160mg | Sodium: 150mg

Roasted Vegetable Breakfast Hash

Prep time: 15 minutes

Cook time: 30 minutes

Servings: 4

Ingredients:

- 2 cups diced sweet potatoes
- 1 cup diced bell peppers (a mix of colors)
- 1 cup diced zucchini
- 1 cup diced red onion
- 1 cup cherry tomatoes
- 3 tablespoons olive oil
- 1 teaspoon dried thyme
- 1 teaspoon paprika
- Salt and pepper to taste
- 4 large eggs
- Fresh parsley, for garnish (optional)

Directions:

1. Preheat the oven to 425°F (220°C) and place a silicon baking mat or several sheets of parchment paper on a baking sheet.
2. Combine the diced sweet potatoes, bell peppers, zucchini, and red onion in a large bowl with the 2 tablespoons of olive oil, dried thyme, paprika, salt, and pepper.
3. Spread the seasoned vegetables on the prepared baking sheet in a single layer.

4. Roast the vegetables in the preheated oven for about 20-25 minutes or until they are tender and lightly browned, stirring once or twice during the roasting process.
5. While the vegetables are roasting, heat the final 1 tablespoon of olive oil in a nonstick skillet over medium heat.
6. After cracking the eggs into the skillet, cook them as desired (for example, fried, sunny-side-up, or over-easy) and season them with salt and pepper.
7. Once the roasted vegetables are done, remove them from the oven and stir in the cherry tomatoes.
8. Divide the Roasted Vegetable Breakfast Hash among four serving plates.
9. Top each plate with a cooked egg and garnish with fresh parsley (if using).
10. Serve the hearty and flavorful Roasted Vegetable Breakfast Hash immediately, and enjoy a nutrient-packed and delicious way to start your day!

Nutritional Info Per Serving
(1/4 of the recipe with one egg):

Calories: 250 | Fats: 14g | Carbs: 25g | Proteins: 9g | Potassium: 700mg | Sodium: 120mg

Almond Butter Banana Toast

✂ *Prep time: 5 minutes*

🍳 *Cook time: 5 minutes*

🍽 *Servings: 2*

🍲 **Ingredients:**

- 2 slices whole-grain bread (or any bread of your choice)
- 2 tablespoons almond butter
- 1 large ripe banana, thinly sliced
- 1 tablespoon honey (optional, for added sweetness)

- 1 tablespoon chia seeds (optional, for extra nutritional value and crunch)
- Pinch of ground cinnamon

🍴 **Directions:**

1. Toast the slices of bread until they are golden and crispy.
2. Spread one tablespoon of almond butter evenly on each slice of toast.
3. Arrange the thinly sliced banana on top of the almond butter, covering the entire surface of each toast.
4. If desired, drizzle honey over the banana slices for added sweetness.
5. Sprinkle chia seeds on top of the banana slices for extra nutrition and a delightful crunch.
6. Finish by dusting a pinch of ground cinnamon over the Almond Butter Banana Toast for added flavor.
7. Serve the delicious and satisfying Almond Butter Banana Toast immediately, and enjoy a quick and nourishing breakfast or snack!
8. Optional variations:
9. Add a sprinkle of granola or crushed nuts for additional texture and flavor.
10. Replace almond butter with peanut butter or any other nut or seed butter you prefer.
11. Use a sprinkle of cocoa powder instead of cinnamon for a chocolatey twist.

Nutritional Info Per Serving
(1 slice of toast):

Calories: 200 | Fats: 10g | Carbs: 26g | Proteins: 5g | Potassium: 310mg | Sodium: 160mg

Chocolate Protein Pancakes

✂ *Prep time: 10 minutes*

🍳 *Cook time: 10 minutes*

🍽 *Servings: 2 (makes about 6 pancakes)*

Ingredients:

- 1 cup whole wheat flour
- 2 tablespoons unsweetened cocoa powder
- 1 scoop chocolate protein powder
- 1 teaspoon baking powder
- 1/4 teaspoon salt
- 1 large egg
- 1 cup unsweetened almond milk (or any milk of your choice)
- 1 tablespoon honey or maple syrup
- 1 teaspoon vanilla extract
- Cooking spray or a little oil for the pan
- Optional toppings:
- Fresh berries
- Sliced bananas
- Greek yogurt
- Drizzle of honey or maple syrup

Directions:

. Whisk the whole wheat flour, unsweetened cocoa powder, chocolate protein powder, baking powder, and salt together in a mixing bowl until thoroughly combined .

. In a different dish, whisk the egg and combine it with the unsweetened almond milk, honey or maple syrup, and vanilla extract.

. Mix the dry ingredients briefly after adding the liquid components. Avoid overmixing; some lumps are acceptable.

. Heat a nonstick skillet or griddle over medium heat while spraying or lightly greasing it.

. For each pancake, add roughly 1/4 cup of batter to the skillet. Cook the pancake until bubbles appear on its surface, then flip it over and continue cooking the second side until it is thoroughly cooked and gently browned.

. Carry out the same procedure with the leftover pancake batter.

7. Stack the Chocolate Protein Pancakes on a serving plate.

8. If you'd like to give the pancakes a little extra sweetness and flavor, you can top them with Greek yogurt, fresh fruit such as banana slices or berries, and a drizzle of honey or maple syrup.

9. Serve the delightful and protein-packed Chocolate Protein Pancakes warm, and enjoy a guilt-free and indulgent breakfast!

Nutritional Info Per Serving (3 pancakes):

Calories: 350 | Fats: 7g | Carbs: 54g | Proteins: 19g | Potassium: 410mg | Sodium: 450mg

Quinoa and Black Bean Breakfast Bowl

Prep time: 15 minutes

Cook time: 20 minutes

Servings: 2

Ingredients:

- 1/2 cup quinoa, rinsed
- 1 cup water or vegetable broth
- 1 cup canned black beans, drained and rinsed
- 1 cup cherry tomatoes, halved
- 1/2 avocado, sliced
- 2 large eggs
- 1 tablespoon olive oil
- 1/2 teaspoon ground cumin
- 1/4 teaspoon paprika
- Salt and pepper to taste
- Fresh cilantro, for garnish (optional)
- Lime wedges, for serving (optional)

Directions:

1. Bring the quinoa and water (or vegetable broth) to a boil in a small saucepan. The quinoa should be cooked and the liquid absorbed after 15 to 20 minutes of simmering on low heat with the lid on.

2. In a nonstick skillet over medium heat, heat the olive oil while the quinoa is cooking.
3. Add the black beans to the skillet and season with salt, pepper, paprika, and ground cumin. The beans should be roasted through and slightly crunchy after 3–4 minutes of cooking.
4. After the quinoa has finished cooking, divide it into two serving bowls and fluff it with a fork.
5. Top the quinoa in each bowl with half of the cooked black beans.
6. In the same skillet, cook the eggs as desired (e.g., fried, sunny-side-up, or over-easy).
7. Place a cooked egg on top of the quinoa and black beans in each bowl.
8. Add the halved cherry tomatoes and sliced avocado to the bowls.
9. Optional: Garnish the Quinoa and Black Bean Breakfast Bowl with fresh cilantro and serve it with lime wedges on the side for a burst of citrus flavor.
10. Serve the hearty and flavorful Quinoa and Black Bean Breakfast Bowl warm, and enjoy a protein-packed and wholesome breakfast to kickstart your day!

Nutritional Info Per Serving:

Calories: 450 | Fats: 19g | Carbs: 51g | Proteins: 21g | Potassium: 820mg | Sodium: 380mg

Lemon Poppy Seed Muffins

🕒 *Prep time: 15 minutes*

🍲 *Cook time: 20 minutes*

🍽 *Servings: 12 muffins*

Ingredients:

- 2 cups all-purpose flour
- 3/4 cup granulated sugar
- 2 tablespoons poppy seeds
- 1 tablespoon baking powder
- 1/4 teaspoon salt
- Zest of 2 lemons
- 1/2 cup unsalted butter, melted
- 1 cup milk (any type you prefer)
- 1/4 cup freshly squeezed lemon juice
- 2 large eggs
- 1 teaspoon vanilla extract
- Optional glaze:
- 1/2 cup powdered sugar
- 1 tablespoon freshly squeezed lemon juice
- 1 teaspoon milk (if needed for desired consistency)

Directions:

1. Set the oven temperature to 375°F (190°C). Grease the cups of a muffin pan with cooking spray or use paper liners.
2. In a big mixing bowl, combine the flour, poppy seeds, brown sugar, baking soda, salt, and lemon zest.
3. Mix the melted butter, milk, lemon juice, eggs, and vanilla extract in a different bowl.
4. After combining them with a spatula, carefully pour the liquid components into the dry ingredients. Avoid overmixing; some lumps are acceptable.
5. Fill each muffin cup with about two-thirds of the muffin batter after dividing it evenly among the prepared muffin cups.
6. When a toothpick put into the center of one of the muffins comes out clean, the lemon poppy seed muffins are done baking.
7. After removing the muffins from the oven, they should cool for a few minutes in the pan before being transferred to a wire rack to finish cooling.
8. Optional glaze:
9. Mix the powdered sugar and freshly squeezed lemon juice in a small bowl until you have a thick glaze. Add a teaspoon of milk at a

time if the glaze is too thick until you have the correct consistency.

10. Once the muffins are completely cooled, drizzle the glaze over the tops of the Lemon Poppy Seed Muffins.

11. Enjoy these delightful and zesty muffins as a delicious breakfast or a sweet treat any time of the day!

Nutritional Info Per Serving (1 muffin):

Calories: 230 | Fats: 9g | Carbs: 33g | Proteins: 4g | Potassium: 70mg | Sodium: 170mg

Cottage Cheese and Berry Bowl

🍽 *Prep time: 5 minutes*

🍲 *Cook time: 0 minutes*

🥘 *Servings: 2*

🍳 **Ingredients:**

1 cup low-fat cottage cheese

- 1 cup mixed berries (e.g., strawberries, blueberries, raspberries)
- 2 tablespoons chopped almonds or walnuts
- 1 tablespoon honey or maple syrup (optional, for added sweetness)
- 1/2 teaspoon vanilla extract
- Optional toppings:
- Fresh mint leaves for garnishing

🍴 **Directions:**

1. Combine low-fat cottage cheese, vanilla extract, and honey or maple syrup (if used) in a mixing blow. Stir thoroughly.

2. Wash the mixed berries and pat them dry with a paper towel. If using strawberries, hull and slice them.

3. Divide the sweetened cottage cheese into two serving bowls.

4. Top each bowl with half of the mixed berries, arranging them over the cottage cheese.

5. Sprinkle chopped almonds or walnuts on top of the berries for added crunch and healthy fats.

6. Optional: Fresh mint leaves can be used to add color and flavor to the Cottage Cheese and Berry Bowl.

7. Serve the refreshing and protein-rich Cottage Cheese and Berry Bowl immediately, and enjoy a delightful and nutritious breakfast or snack!

Nutritional Info Per Serving:

Calories: 180 | Fats: 6g | Carbs: 19g | Proteins: 14g | Potassium: 220mg | Sodium: 360mg

Baked Egg Avocado Boats

🍽 *Prep time: 10 minutes*

🍲 *Cook time: 15 minutes*

🥘 *Servings: 2*

🍳 **Ingredients:**

- 1 large ripe avocado
- 2 large eggs
- Salt and pepper to taste
- 1 tablespoon chopped fresh herbs (e.g., parsley, chives, or cilantro) for garnish
- Optional toppings:
- Crushed red pepper flakes
- Shredded cheese (e.g., cheddar or feta)
- Diced tomatoes
- Cooked and crumbled bacon

🍴 **Directions:**

1. Set your oven temperature to 375°F (190°C).

2. Cut the ripe avocado in half and remove the pit. Using a spoon, scoop out a little extra flesh from each avocado half to create a larger space for the egg.

3. To ensure that the avocado halves won't fall over while baking, place

them in a baking dish or on a baking sheet.

4. Crack one egg into each avocado half, being careful not to overflow it. If the avocado halves have a small cavity, you can remove a little egg white to fit it better.
5. Sprinkle salt and pepper over the eggs.
6. Optional: Add toppings like shredded cheese, crushed red pepper flakes, diced tomatoes, or cooked and crumbled bacon on top of the eggs.
7. Bake the Baked Egg Avocado Boats in the preheated oven for about 15 minutes or until the egg whites are set, but the yolks are still slightly runny. If you prefer the yolks fully cooked, you can bake them a few minutes longer.
8. Once the eggs are cooked to your desired doneness, remove the avocado boats from the oven.
9. Garnish the Baked Egg Avocado Boats with chopped fresh herbs (parsley, chives, or cilantro) for added flavor and freshness.
10. Serve the delicious and nutritious Baked Egg Avocado Boats immediately while they are warm, and enjoy a protein-packed and satisfying breakfast or brunch!

Nutritional Info Per Serving
(1 avocado half with one egg):

Calories: 180 | Fats: 15g | Carbs: 6g | Proteins: 7g | Potassium: 450mg | Sodium: 65mg

Pomegranate and Pistachio Yogurt Parfait

🍴 *Prep time: 10 minutes*

🍲 *Cook time: 0 minutes*

🍽 *Servings: 2*

Ingredients:

- 1 cup Greek yogurt (plain or vanilla flavored)
- 1/2 cup pomegranate arils (seeds)
- 1/4 cup chopped pistachios
- 2 tablespoons honey or maple syrup (optional, for added sweetness)
- 1/2 teaspoon vanilla extract
- Optional toppings:
- Fresh mint leaves for garnish

Directions:

1. Greek yogurt, honey or maple syrup (if using), and vanilla extract should all be combined in a bowl. Mix the flavors together thoroughly.
2. Wash the pomegranate and cut it in half. Gently remove the arils (seeds) and set them aside.
3. Chop the pistachios into small pieces.
4. In two serving glasses or parfait cups, layer the Greek yogurt, pomegranate arils, and chopped pistachios.
5. Continue layering until you have used all the ingredients, finishing with a layer of pomegranate arils and a sprinkle of chopped pistachios on top.
6. Optional: For a splash of color and a revitalizing scent, add fresh mint leaves to the Pomegranate and Pistachio Yogurt Parfait's garnish.
7. Serve the delightful and nutrient-rich Pomegranate and Pistachio Yogurt Parfait immediately, and enjoy a refreshing and indulgent breakfast or dessert!

Nutritional Info Per Serving:

Calories: 250 | Fats: 11g | Carbs: 27g | Proteins: 13g | Potassium: 320mg | Sodium: 70mg

Cinnamon Raisin French Toast

🍳 *Prep time: 10 minutes*

🍲 *Cook time: 10 minutes*

🍽 *Servings: 2*

🥄 Ingredients:

- 4 slices of whole-grain bread
- 2 large eggs
- 1/2 cup milk (any type you prefer)
- 1 teaspoon ground cinnamon
- 1/2 teaspoon vanilla extract
- 1/4 cup raisins
- Cooking spray or a little butter for the pan
- Maple syrup or honey, for serving
- Fresh berries, for garnish (optional)

📋 Directions:

1. Stir the eggs, milk, ground cinnamon, and vanilla extract until completely incorporated in a shallow dish or bowl.
2. Make sure both sides of each piece of whole-grain bread are coated in the egg mixture. Give the bread about 30 seconds on each side to absorb the ingredients.
3. Sprinkle raisins on top of two of the soaked bread slices.
4. Place the soaked bread slices with raisins on top of the plain soaked bread slices to form two "sandwiches."
5. Melt a little butter nonstick skillet or griddle over medium heat, or spray it with cooking spray.
6. Place the "sandwiches" on the skillet and cook them for about 3-4 minutes on each side until they are golden brown and crispy.
7. Once both sides are cooked to perfection, remove the Cinnamon Raisin French Toast from the skillet.
8. Cut each "sandwich" diagonally to form four triangle-shaped pieces.
9. Optional: Garnish the French toast with fresh berries for added color and nutrition.
10. Serve the warm and delicious Cinnamon Raisin French Toast with maple syrup or honey drizzled on top, and enjoy a delightful and comforting breakfast!

Nutritional Info Per Serving
(2 slices of French toast):

Calories: 350 | Fats: 9g | Carbs: 55g | Proteins: 13g | Potassium: 350mg | Sodium: 360mg

Lunch Recipes

Lemon Herb Grilled Turkey Burgers

🎋 *Prep time: 15 minutes*

🍲 *Cook time: 15 minutes*

🍽 *Servings: 4 burgers*

🥄 **Ingredients:**

- 1 pound ground turkey (preferably lean)
- 1 tablespoon fresh lemon juice
- 1 tablespoon olive oil
- 1 teaspoon lemon zest
- 1 tablespoon chopped fresh parsley
- 1 tablespoon chopped fresh basil
- 1 teaspoon minced garlic
- 1/2 teaspoon dried oregano
- 1/2 teaspoon dried thyme
- Salt and pepper to taste
- 4 whole wheat burger buns
- Topping of lettuce leaves, tomato slices, and red onion slices (optional)

📋 **Directions:**

1. Combine the ground turkey with the fresh lemon juice, olive oil, lemon zest, fresh parsley, fresh basil, minced garlic, dried oregano, dried thyme, salt, and pepper in a large mixing bowl. Mix everything thoroughly to incorporate each ingredient.
2. Split the turkey mixture evenly into four parts.
3. Form each portion into a patty that is roughly 1/2 inch thick and a little bigger than the size of your burger buns because the patties will somewhat shrink when cooking.
4. Bring up the heat on your grill or grill pan.
5. Lightly grease the grill with a little oil or cooking spray to prevent sticking.
6. By the time the turkey burgers are placed on the grill and cooked for about 6-7 minutes on each side, they should be well done and have an internal temperature of 165°F (74°C).
7. During the last minute of cooking, you can place the whole wheat burger buns on the grill to toast them slightly.
8. When the turkey burgers have finished cooking, take them off the grill and give them a moment to rest.
9. Assemble your Lemon Herb Grilled Turkey Burgers by placing each patty on a whole wheat burger bun. Add optional toppings like lettuce leaves, tomato slices, and red onion slices for extra flavor and crunch.
10. Serve the delicious and lean Lemon Herb Grilled Turkey Burgers, and enjoy a healthy and savory lunch that's satisfying and DASH diet-friendly!

Nutritional Info Per Serving
(1 burger without toppings):

Calories: 250 | Fats: 12g | Carbs: 19g | Proteins: 18g | Potassium: 260mg | Sodium: 230mg

Lemon Garlic Shrimp and Asparagus Stir Fry

🎋 *Prep time: 10 minutes*

🍲 *Cook time: 10 minutes*

🍽 *Servings: 4*

🥄 **Ingredients:**

- 1 pound large shrimp, peeled and deveined
- 1 bunch asparagus, trimmed and cut into bite-sized pieces
- 3 cloves garlic, minced
- 2 tablespoons olive oil
- Zest of 1 lemon
- Juice of 1 lemon

- 1 tablespoon low-sodium soy sauce
- 1 teaspoon honey (optional, for a touch of sweetness)
- Salt and pepper to taste
- Red pepper flakes (optional, for added spice)
- Cooked brown rice or quinoa, for serving

Directions:

1. The lemon garlic sauce is made by combining minced garlic, olive oil, lemon zest, lemon juice, low-sodium soy sauce, honey (if used), salt, and pepper in a small bowl. Set aside.
2. Heat 1 tablespoon of olive oil to medium-high heat in a large skillet or wok.
3. Add the shrimp to the skillet and cook them for about 1-2 minutes on each side until they turn pink and opaque. Remove the shrimp from the skillet and set them aside.
4. Fill the same skillet with the last tablespoon of olive oil.
5. Add the asparagus to the skillet and stir-fry them for about 3-4 minutes until they are tender-crisp.
6. Return the cooked shrimp to the skillet, and pour the lemon garlic sauce over the shrimp and asparagus.
7. Toss everything together until the shrimp and asparagus are coated evenly with the sauce. If you prefer a little heat, sprinkle some red pepper flakes over the stir fry and toss again.
8. Once everything is heated through and well combined, remove the skillet from the heat.
9. Serve the delectable Lemon Garlic Shrimp and Asparagus Stir Fry over cooked brown rice or quinoa for a nutritious and flavorful meal.

Nutritional Info Per Serving
(1/4 of the recipe, excluding rice/quinoa):

Calories: 220 | Fats: 10g | Carbs: 6g | Proteins: 27g | Potassium: 450mg | Sodium: 290mg

Mediterranean Chickpea Salad

Prep time: 15 minutes
Cook time: 0 minutes
Servings: 4

Ingredients:

- 2 cups cooked chickpeas (canned or homemade)
- 1 cup cherry tomatoes, halved
- 1 cucumber, diced
- 1/2 red bell pepper, diced
- 1/4 red onion, finely chopped
- 1/2 cup Kalamata olives, pitted and halved
- 1/3 cup crumbled feta cheese
- 1/4 cup chopped fresh parsley
- 1/4 cup chopped fresh mint
- 3 tablespoons extra-virgin olive oil
- 2 tablespoons red wine vinegar
- 1 clove garlic, minced
- Salt and pepper to taste
- Lemon wedges, for serving (optional)
- Pita bread or whole wheat tortillas, for serving (optional)

Directions:

1. Combine the cooked chickpeas, halved Kalamata olives, cherry tomatoes, diced cucumber, diced red bell pepper, finely chopped red onion, chopped fresh parsley, and chopped fresh mint in a large mixing bowl.
2. The dressing is made by combining extra virgin olive oil, red wine vinegar, garlic, salt, and pepper in a small bowl.

3. Spoon the dressing over the components of the chickpea salad in the big mixing bowl.
4. Toss everything together until all the ingredients are well coated with the dressing.
5. Taste the chickpea salad and, if necessary, add additional salt and pepper to taste.
6. Optional: Serve the salad with lemon wedges on the side for an extra burst of citrus flavor.
7. Serve the delightful and refreshing Mediterranean Chickpea Salad on its own as a light and satisfying meal or as a side dish for grilled chicken, fish, or meat.
8. If desired, serve the salad wrapped in pita bread or whole wheat tortillas for a delicious and portable lunch option.

Nutritional Info Per Serving
(1/4 of the recipe, excluding optional serving items):

Calories: 320 | Fats: 16g | Carbs: 35g | Proteins: 10g | Potassium: 430mg | Sodium: 580mg

Grilled Lemon Herb Chicken

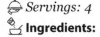 *Prep time: 10 minutes*

(+ marinating time)

Cook time: 15 minutes

Servings: 4

Ingredients:

- 4 boneless, skinless chicken breasts
- Juice of 2 lemons
- Zest of 1 lemon
- 3 tablespoons olive oil
- 2 cloves garlic, minced
- 1 tablespoon chopped fresh thyme
- 1 tablespoon chopped fresh rosemary
- 1 tablespoon chopped fresh parsley
- 1/2 teaspoon dried oregano
- 1/2 teaspoon dried basil
- Salt and pepper to taste
- Lemon wedges and fresh herbs for garnish (optional)

Directions:

1. To make the marinade, mix the lemon juice, lemon zest, olive oil, minced garlic, fresh thyme, rosemary, and parsley, as well as the dried oregano and basil, salt, and pepper in a bowl.
2. Place the chicken breasts on a shallow dish or in a sealable plastic bag.
3. Cover all of the chicken with the marinade, making sure to coat every piece. To ensure that the marinade is applied evenly, knead the chicken with your hands as you add the marinade.
4. The chicken should be marinated in the fridge for at least an hour, but ideally overnight to allow the flavors to mingle. Seal the bag or cover the dish.
5. Preheat your grill to medium-high heat.
6. Take the chicken out of the marinade and discard the liquid.
7. The internal temperature of the chicken breasts must reach 165°F (74°C) by grilling them for 6-7 minutes on each side.
8. Once the chicken is grilled to perfection, remove it from the grill and let it rest for a couple of minutes before serving.
9. Optional: Garnish the Grilled Lemon Herb Chicken with lemon wedges and fresh herbs for an extra touch of citrusy and herbal freshness.
10. Serve the delectable and flavorful Grilled Lemon Herb Chicken as a delightful main course, and enjoy a scrumptious and protein-rich meal

Turkey and Quinoa Stuffed Zucchini Boats

⅔ *Prep time: 20 minutes*

🍳 *Cook time: 30 minutes*

🍲 *Servings: 4 zucchini boats*

Ingredients:

- 2 large zucchinis
- 1/2 cup uncooked quinoa
- 1 cup water or vegetable broth
- 1 tablespoon olive oil
- 1/2 pound ground turkey
- 1/2 onion, finely chopped
- 2 cloves garlic, minced
- 1 teaspoon ground cumin
- 1 teaspoon paprika
- 1/2 teaspoon dried oregano
- 1/2 teaspoon dried basil
- Salt and pepper to taste
- 1 cup diced tomatoes (canned or fresh)
- 1/4 cup shredded mozzarella or feta cheese (optional, for topping)
- Fresh parsley or cilantro, for garnish (optional)

Directions:

1. Set the oven temperature to 375°F (190°C).
2. After cutting the zucchinis lengthwise, scoop out the seeds and some of the flesh with a spoon to create a cavity for the filling. Keep the zucchini flesh you've removed for later.
3. In a fine-mesh strainer, rinse the quinoa under cold water.
4. Place the rinsed quinoa in a small pot with water or vegetable broth. Bring the liquid to a boil quickly over high heat. As soon as it starts to boil, reduce the heat to low, cover the pan, and simmer the quinoa for around 15 minutes, or until all the liquid has been absorbed. Once you've removed it from the flame, fluff it with a fork.
5. Place a large skillet over medium heat and warm the olive oil.
6. Add the ground turkey, minced garlic, and finely diced onion to the skillet. Cook the turkey until it is browned and well done, breaking it up with a spatula as you go. Drain any fat.
7. Add the reserved zucchini flesh to the skillet with the turkey mixture.
8. Stir in the ground cumin, paprika, dried oregano, dried basil, salt, and pepper. Cook everything together for another 2-3 minutes until the flavors are well combined.
9. Add the diced tomatoes and cooked quinoa to the turkey mixture in the skillet. Stir everything together until it forms a well-mixed filling.
10. Place the hollowed zucchini halves in a baking dish or on a baking sheet.
11. Spoon the turkey and quinoa filling into each zucchini half, pressing it down slightly to pack the filling.
12. Optional: Sprinkle shredded mozzarella or feta cheese on top of each stuffed zucchini boat for added richness.
13. Bake the Turkey and Quinoa Stuffed Zucchini Boats in the preheated oven for about 20-25 minutes or until the zucchini is tender and the filling is heated through.
14. When the zucchini boats are done baking, remove them from the oven and let them cool a little.
15. Optional: Garnish the stuffed zucchini boats with fresh parsley or cilantro for a burst of herbal freshness.
16. Serve the delectable and wholesome Turkey and Quinoa Stuffed Zucchini Boats as a fantastic

and nourishing main course, and enjoy a well-balanced and flavorful meal!

Lemon Dill Salmon with Steamed Broccoli

Prep time: 10 minutes

Cook time: 15 minutes

Servings: 4

Ingredients:

- 4 salmon fillets (about 6 ounces each), skin-on or skinless
- Zest of 1 lemon
- Juice of 1 lemon
- 2 tablespoons olive oil
- 2 cloves garlic, minced
- 1 tablespoon chopped fresh dill
- Salt and pepper to taste
- 1 pound broccoli florets
- Lemon wedges for serving (optional)

Directions:

1. Set the oven temperature to 375°F (190°C).
2. In a small bowl, combine the lemon zest, lemon juice, olive oil, minced garlic, fresh dill, salt, and pepper to prepare the lemon dill marinade.
3. Put the salmon fillets in a sealable plastic bag or a shallow dish.
4. Pour the lemon dill marinade over the salmon, making sure each fillet is coated. You can use your hands to gently rub the marinade into the salmon.
5. Leave the salmon to marinate in the refrigerator for about 30 minutes with the lid or bag closed to help the flavors meld.

6. While the salmon is marinating, prepare the broccoli by steaming it until it's tender-crisp. You can steam it on the stovetop using a steamer basket or in the microwave.
7. A big oven-safe skillet should be preheated on medium-high.
8. Take the salmon out of the marinade and discard the marinade.
9. If using salmon fillets with skin on, place them skin-side down in the heating skillet.
10. Sear the salmon for about 2-3 minutes on each side until they have a golden crust.
11. The Lemon Dill Salmon should be baked for 8 to 10 minutes, or until it is cooked through and flakes readily with a fork, after being seared.
12. While the salmon is baking, prepare the steamed broccoli for serving.
13. Once the salmon is done, remove the skillet from the oven and let the salmon rest for a minute.
14. Serve the succulent and flavorful Lemon Dill Salmon with Steamed Broccoli on a plate, and garnish with lemon wedges if desired.
15. Enjoy the nutritious and delightful Lemon Dill Salmon with the tender-crisp Steamed Broccoli for a wholesome and satisfying meal!

Veggie Fajita Lettuce Wraps

Prep time: 15 minutes

Cook time: 15 minutes

Servings: 4 lettuce wraps

Ingredients:

- 1 tablespoon olive oil
- 1 red bell pepper, thinly sliced
- 1 yellow bell pepper, thinly sliced
- 1 green bell pepper, thinly sliced
- 1 onion, thinly sliced
- 1 zucchini, thinly sliced
- 1 cup corn kernels (fresh, frozen, or canned)
- 2 cloves garlic, minced
- 1 teaspoon ground cumin
- 1 teaspoon chili powder
- 1/2 teaspoon paprika
- Salt and pepper to taste
- 1 tablespoon lime juice
- 1/4 cup chopped fresh cilantro
- 8 large lettuce leaves (such as romaine or butter lettuce)
- Optional toppings:
- Avocado slices
- Salsa
- Greek yogurt or sour cream

Directions:

1. Over medium-high heat, preheat the olive oil in a big skillet.
2. Add the thinly sliced red, yellow, and green onions and bell peppers. Cook to soften for 3 to 4 minutes, stirring periodically.
3. Add the thinly sliced zucchini and corn kernels to the skillet. Continue to cook for another 3-4 minutes until all the vegetables are tender-crisp.
4. Add the garlic powder, salt, pepper, paprika, chili powder, and cumin powder. Cook the vegetables for another minute while tossing regularly, or until they are soft and the spices are fragrant.
5. Turn off the heat and drizzle the lime juice over the veggie fajita mixture. Toss everything together to coat the veggies with the lime juice.
6. Sprinkle the chopped fresh cilantro over the fajita mixture and give it a final toss.
7. To assemble the Veggie Fajita Lettuce Wraps, take a large lettuce leaf and spoon a generous amount of the veggie fajita mixture onto the center of the leaf.
8. Optional: To add richness and flavor to the veggie mixture, add avocado slices, salsa, and a dollop of Greek yogurt or sour cream.
9. Fold the sides of the lettuce leaf over the filling, and then roll it up like a burrito.
10. Repeat the process with the remaining lettuce leaves and veggie fajita mixture to make a total of 4 lettuce wraps.
11. Serve the delightful and nutritious Veggie Fajita Lettuce Wraps as a light and wholesome meal, and enjoy the colorful and flavorful combination of vegetables wrapped in fresh lettuce leaves!

Nutritional Info Per Serving
(1 lettuce wrap, excluding optional toppings):

Calories: 120 | Fats: 5g | Carbs: 18g | Proteins: 4g | Potassium: 420mg | Sodium: 40mg

Baked Cod with Herbed Quinoa

Prep time: 15 minutes

Cook time: 25 minutes

Servings: 4

Ingredients:

- For the Baked Cod:
- 4 cod fillets (about 6 ounces each)
- 2 tablespoons olive oil

- Juice of 1 lemon
- 2 cloves garlic, minced
- 1 teaspoon dried oregano
- 1 teaspoon dried thyme
- 1 teaspoon dried rosemary
- Salt and pepper to taste
- For the Herbed Quinoa:
- 1 cup quinoa, rinsed
- 2 cups vegetable broth or water
- 1 tablespoon chopped fresh parsley
- 1 tablespoon chopped fresh dill
- 1 tablespoon chopped fresh chives
- Salt and pepper to taste
- For Serving (optional):
- Lemon wedges
- Steamed vegetables (such as broccoli or asparagus)

⊠ Directions:

1. Set the oven temperature to 375°F (190°C).
2. To prepare the marinade for the cod, combine the olive oil, lemon juice, minced garlic, dried oregano, dried thyme, dried rosemary, salt, and pepper in a small bowl.
3. Put the cod fillets in a sealable plastic bag or a shallow dish.
4. Pour the marinade over the cod fillets, making sure each fillet is coated. You can gently rub the marinade into the cod to ensure that it is evenly distributed.
5. To enable the flavors to meld, cover the dish or seal the bag and place the fish in the refrigerator for about 15 minutes.
6. While the cod is marinating, prepare the herbed quinoa. Mix the rinsed quinoa with water or vegetable broth in a saucepan. Bring the mixture to a boil over medium-high heat. Once it begins to boil, immediately reduce the heat to low, cover the pan, and let the quinoa simmer for about 15 minutes, or until the liquid is absorbed and the quinoa is cooked.
7. With a fork, fluff the cooked quinoa after it is done cooking, then season with salt, pepper, fresh chives, fresh dill, and fresh parsley. The quinoa should be completely mixed with all of the other ingredients.
8. Preheat a big oven-safe skillet on medium-high.
9. Remove the cod from the marinade, and discard the marinade.
10. Place the cod fillets in the preheated skillet, and sear them for about 2-3 minutes on each side until they have a golden crust.
11. Once seared, transfer the skillet to the preheated oven and bake the cod for about 10-12 minutes or until it's cooked through and flakes easily with a fork.
12. While the cod is baking, you can steam your choice of vegetables to serve as a side dish.
13. Once the cod is done, remove the skillet from the oven and let the cod rest for a minute.
14. Serve the tender and flavorful Baked Cod with a side of Herbed Quinoa, and garnish with lemon wedges if desired.
15. Optional: Serve steamed vegetables alongside the Baked Cod and Herbed Quinoa for a wholesome and well-balanced meal.
16. Enjoy the nutritious and delectable Baked Cod with Herbed Quinoa for a delightful and wholesome dinner!

Nutritional Info Per Serving
(1 cod fillet with 1/4 of the herbed quinoa, excluding optional items):
Calories: 400 | Fats: 14g | Carbs: 30g | Proteins: 35g | Potassium: 790mg | Sodium: 220mg

Greek Yogurt Chicken Salad Lettuce Wraps

Prep time: 15 minutes

Cook time: 20 minutes

(if using cooked chicken)

Servings: 4 lettuce wraps

Ingredients:

- 2 cups cooked and shredded chicken breast (rotisserie or grilled chicken works well)
- 1/2 cup Greek yogurt (plain, non-fat or low-fat)
- 1/4 cup diced cucumber
- 1/4 cup diced red bell pepper
- 1/4 cup diced red onion
- 1/4 cup halved cherry tomatoes
- 1/4 cup pitted Kalamata olives, chopped
- 2 tablespoons chopped fresh parsley
- 1 tablespoon chopped fresh dill
- 1 tablespoon lemon juice
- 1 tablespoon extra-virgin olive oil
- 1 clove garlic, minced
- Salt and pepper to taste
- 4 large lettuce leaves (such as romaine or butter lettuce)
- Optional toppings:
- Crumbled feta cheese
- Sliced black olives
- Sliced cucumber
- Lemon wedges

Directions:

1. In a big mixing bowl, add the Greek yogurt, diced cucumber, red bell pepper, red onion, cherry tomatoes, chopped Kalamata olives, chopped fresh parsley, and chopped fresh dill.
2. In a separate small bowl, whisk together the lemon juice, extra-virgin olive oil, minced garlic, salt, and pepper to create the dressing.
3. Pour the dressing over the chicken salad ingredients in the large mixing bowl.
4. Toss everything together until the chicken and vegetables are well coated with the dressing.
5. Taste the Greek yogurt chicken salad and season with more salt and pepper if desired.
6. To assemble the lettuce wraps, take a large lettuce leaf and spoon a generous amount of the Greek Yogurt Chicken Salad onto the center of the leaf.
7. Optional: Add crumbled feta cheese, sliced black olives, sliced cucumber, and a squeeze of fresh lemon juice on top of the chicken salad for extra Mediterranean flavors.
8. Fold the sides of the lettuce leaf over the filling, and then roll it up like a burrito.
9. Repeat the process with the remaining lettuce leaves and Greek Yogurt Chicken Salad to make a total of 4 lettuce wraps.
10. Serve the delightful and protein-packed Greek Yogurt Chicken Salad Lettuce Wraps as a refreshing and light meal, and enjoy the Mediterranean-inspired flavors wrapped in fresh lettuce leaves!

Nutritional Info Per Serving
(1 lettuce wrap, excluding optional toppings):

Calories: 220 | Fats: 9g | Carbs: 6g | Proteins: 28g | Potassium: 520mg | Sodium: 270mg

Cauliflower Rice and Black Bean Burrito Bowl

Prep time: 15 minutes

Cook time: 20 minutes

Servings: 4

Ingredients:

- 1 medium head of cauliflower,

riced (or 4 cups store-bought cauliflower rice)

- 1 tablespoon olive oil
- 1 small onion, diced
- 1 red bell pepper, diced
- 1 cup cooked black beans (canned or homemade)
- 1 cup corn kernels (fresh, frozen, or canned)
- 1 teaspoon ground cumin
- 1 teaspoon chili powder
- 1/2 teaspoon smoked paprika
- Salt and pepper to taste
- Juice of 1 lime
- 1/4 cup chopped fresh cilantro
- 1 avocado, sliced (for serving)
- Greek yogurt or sour cream (for serving)
- Salsa (for serving)

✂ Directions:

1. To make your own cauliflower rice, separate the cauliflower florets and pulse them in a food processor until they resemble rice grains. Making your own cauliflower rice is more cost-effective than purchasing it. The cauliflower might also be grated using a box grater.
2. Warm up the olive oil in a big skillet over medium heat.
3. Add the diced red bell pepper and onion to the skillet. They should be sautéed for 3 to 4 minutes until they soften.
4. Stir in the cauliflower rice after adding it to the skillet.
5. Sprinkle the ground cumin, chili powder, smoked paprika, salt, and pepper over the cauliflower rice. Stir to coat the rice and veggies with the spices.
6. Add the cooked black beans and corn kernels to the skillet. Stir again until everything is well combined.
7. Squeeze the lime juice over the burrito bowl mixture, and toss everything together.

8. Cook the Cauliflower Rice and Black Bean Burrito Bowl for another 3-4 minutes, or until the cauliflower rice is cooked to your desired texture.
9. Turn off the heat, and sprinkle the chopped fresh cilantro over the burrito bowl. Toss everything one last time to incorporate the cilantro
10. To serve, divide the Cauliflower Rice and Black Bean Burrito Bowl into individual serving bowls.
11. For extra richness and flavor, top each bowl with a heaping spoonful of salsa, a slice of avocado, and a dollop of sour cream or Greek yogurt.
12. Enjoy the wholesome and flavorful Cauliflower Rice and Black Bean Burrito Bowl as a delicious and nutritious vegetarian meal!

Nutritional Info Per Serving
(1/4 of the recipe, excluding optional toppings):

Calories: 210 | Fats: 9g | Carbs: 28g | Proteins: 8g | Potassium: 550mg | Sodium: 190mg

Teriyaki Tofu and Veggie Skewers

🥬 *Prep time: 20 minutes*

(+ marinating time)

🍲 *Cook time: 15 minutes*

🍽 *Servings: 4 skewers*

🍽 Ingredients:

- 1 block of firm tofu, pressed and cut into cubes
- 1 red bell pepper, cut into chunks
- 1 green bell pepper, cut into chunks
- 1 zucchini, sliced into rounds
- 1 cup cherry tomatoes
- 1/4 cup low-sodium soy sauce c tamari (for a gluten-free option
- 2 tablespoons water

- 2 tablespoons honey or maple syrup (for a vegan option)
- 1 tablespoon rice vinegar
- 1 tablespoon sesame oil
- 1 teaspoon grated fresh ginger
- 2 cloves garlic, minced
- 1 tablespoon sesame seeds (optional, for garnish)
- Sliced green onions (optional, for garnish)
- Cooked quinoa or rice, for serving (optional)

✂ Directions:

1. In a bowl, whisk together the low-sodium soy sauce or tamari, water, honey or maple syrup, rice vinegar, sesame oil, grated fresh ginger, and minced garlic to create the teriyaki marinade.
2. Put the tofu cubes in a zip-top bag or on a shallow plate.
3. Pour half of the teriyaki marinade over the tofu, making sure the tofu is well coated. Reserve the other half of the marinade for later.
4. To allow the flavors to meld, place the tofu in the refrigerator and cover the dish or seal the bag. This should be done for at least 30 minutes and ideally for 1-2 hours.
5. To avoid having wooden skewers burn while grilling, soak them in water for about 20 minutes.
6. Preheat your grill to medium-high heat.
7. Skewer the marinated tofu cubes, along with the red and green bell pepper chunks, zucchini slices, and cherry tomatoes, alternating the ingredients for a colorful presentation.
8. Brush the vegetable skewers with the reserved teriyaki marinade to give them extra flavor.
9. Place the Teriyaki Tofu and Veggie Skewers on the preheated grill, and cook for about 6-8 minutes on each side, or until the tofu and

vegetables are lightly charred and cooked to your liking.
10. Optional: Sprinkle sesame seeds over the skewers for added crunch and flavor, and garnish with sliced green onions.
11. Serve the delectable Teriyaki Tofu and Veggie Skewers on their own as a mouthwatering vegan dish, or pair them with cooked quinoa or rice for a wholesome and balanced meal.
12. Enjoy the scrumptious and protein-rich Teriyaki Tofu and Veggie Skewers for a delightful and satisfying dining experience!

Nutritional Info Per Serving
(1 skewer, excluding optional items and side):

Calories: 160 | Fats: 6g | Carbs: 19g | Proteins: 9g | Potassium: 410mg | Sodium: 290mg

Spaghetti Squash with Turkey Bolognese

🍳 *Prep time: 15 minutes*

🍲 *Cook time: 1 hour 15 minutes*

🍽 *Servings: 4*

🥢 Ingredients:

- 1 medium spaghetti squash
- 1 tablespoon olive oil
- 1 pound ground turkey
- 1 small onion, finely chopped
- 2 cloves garlic, minced
- 1 carrot, peeled and finely chopped
- 1 celery stalk, finely chopped
- 1 can (14 ounces) crushed tomatoes
- 1 can (6 ounces) tomato paste
- 1 teaspoon dried oregano
- 1 teaspoon dried basil
- 1/2 teaspoon dried thyme
- Salt and pepper to taste
- Fresh basil leaves, for garnish (optional)
- Grated Parmesan cheese, for serving (optional)

Directions:

1. Set the oven to 400 °F (200 °C).
2. Split the spaghetti squash in half lengthwise with care. Remove the squash's seeds and stringy inside using a spoon.
3. Sprinkle each squash half's interior with salt and pepper and spray it with olive oil. Place the halves on a parchment-lined baking sheet, cut-side down.
4. Roast the spaghetti squash for 45 to 50 minutes in a preheated oven, or until the flesh is fork-tender and easily separates. Take it out of the oven, then allow it to cool slightly.
5. While the spaghetti squash roasts, prepare the turkey Bolognese sauce. In a large skillet, heat the olive oil to a medium-high temperature.
6. Stir in the ground turkey and heat it in the skillet until it is thoroughly cooked and browned. Use a spatula to separate it as it cooks.
7. Add the finely chopped onion, minced garlic, chopped carrot, and chopped celery to the skillet with the cooked turkey. Cook everything together for about 5 minutes until the vegetables are tender.
8. After adding the dried oregano, dried basil, dried thyme, and tomato paste, salt, and pepper, stir in the smashed tomatoes and tomato paste. Mix everything thoroughly to form the sauce.
9. Allow the turkey Bolognese sauce to simmer for about 15-20 minutes, allowing the flavors to blend, on low heat with a lid on the skillet.
10. Once the spaghetti squash is done roasting and has cooled slightly, use a fork to scrape the flesh into spaghetti-like strands.
11. To serve, divide the spaghetti squash strands among individual serving plates.
12. Top each plate of spaghetti squash with a generous amount of the turkey Bolognese sauce.
13. Optional: For extra herbal freshness and savory goodness, garnish each plate with fresh basil leaves and a sprinkling of grated Parmesan cheese.
14. Enjoy the wholesome and flavorful Spaghetti Squash with Turkey Bolognese as a satisfying and nutritious meal!

Nutritional Info Per Serving
(1/4 of the recipe, excluding optional items):

Calories: 340 | Fats: 15g | Carbs: 25g | Proteins: 28g | Potassium: 820mg | Sodium: 520mg

Quinoa and Roasted Vegetable Buddha Bowl

Prep time: 15 minutes

Cook time: 30 minutes

Servings: 4 bowls

Ingredients:

- 1 cup quinoa, rinsed
- 2 cups vegetable broth or water
- 1 medium sweet potato, peeled and diced
- 1 red bell pepper, diced
- 1 zucchini, diced
- 1 cup cherry tomatoes
- 1 tablespoon olive oil
- 1 teaspoon ground cumin
- 1 teaspoon smoked paprika
- Salt and pepper to taste
- 2 cups baby spinach or mixed greens
- 1 avocado, sliced
- 1/4 cup crumbled feta cheese (optional, for serving)
- Lemon wedges (for serving)
- Balsamic glaze or dressing of choice (for serving)

Directions:

1. After being rinsed, heat the quinoa with either water or vegetable broth. Bring the liquid to a quick boil over high heat. Once the

quinoa starts to boil, turn the heat down to low, cover the pan, and simmer the quinoa for 15 to 20 minutes, or until the liquid is absorbed and the quinoa is cooked.

2. Set the oven temperature to 400 °F (200 °C).

3. Combine the diced sweet potato, red bell pepper, zucchini, and cherry tomatoes with the olive oil, cumin powder, smoked paprika, salt, and pepper on a baking sheet.

4. Arrange the seasoned vegetables on the baking sheet in a single layer.

5. Roast the vegetables in the preheated oven for about 20-25 minutes or until they are tender and lightly caramelized, stirring halfway through.

6. Once the quinoa and roasted vegetables are done, you can start assembling the Buddha bowls.

7. In each bowl, start with a bed of baby spinach or mixed greens.

8. Spoon a generous amount of cooked quinoa over the greens.

9. Top the quinoa with a serving of roasted vegetables.

10. Add the sliced avocado and crumbled feta cheese on top of the veggies for added creaminess and flavor (optional).

11. Drizzle your favorite balsamic glaze or dressing over the Quinoa and Roasted Vegetable Buddha Bowls.

12. Squeeze fresh lemon juice over each bowl for a refreshing touch.

13. Enjoy the nourishing and colorful Quinoa and Roasted Vegetable Buddha Bowl for a well-rounded and delightful meal!

Nutritional Info Per Serving
(1/4 of the recipe, excluding optional items and dressing):

Calories: 330 | Fats: 13g | Carbs: 47g | Proteins: 9g | Potassium: 820mg | Sodium: 210mg

Cilantro Lime Shrimp Tacos

🍴 *Prep time: 15 minutes*

🍲 *Cook time: 10 minutes*

🍽 *Servings: 4 tacos*

🥄 **Ingredients:**

- For the Cilantro Lime Shrimp:
- 1 pound large shrimp, peeled and deveined
- Zest of 1 lime
- Juice of 2 limes
- 2 tablespoons olive oil
- 2 cloves garlic, minced
- 1 teaspoon ground cumin
- 1/2 teaspoon chili powder
- 1/4 teaspoon cayenne pepper (optional, for heat)
- Salt and pepper to taste
- 1/4 cup chopped fresh cilantro
- For Assembling the Tacos:
- 8 small corn tortillas
- Shredded lettuce or cabbage
- Sliced avocado or guacamole
- Sliced red onion
- Sliced jalapeño (optional, for heat)
- Additional chopped fresh cilantro
- Lime wedges

🍳 **Directions:**

1. In a medium bowl, mix the peeled and deveined shrimp with olive oil, chopped garlic, ground cumin, chili powder, cayenne pepper (if used), salt, and pepper.

2. Toss the shrimp in the marinade until they are well coated. Let the shrimp marinate in the refrigerator for about 10 minutes to allow the flavors to infuse.

3. Preheat a large skillet over medium-high heat.

4. Add the marinated shrimp to the preheated skillet and cook them for about 2-3 minutes on each side or until they are pink and cooked through. Be careful not to overcook

the shrimp to keep them tender and juicy.

5. Once the shrimp are done, remove the skillet from the heat and stir in the chopped fresh cilantro.

6. Briefly warm the corn tortillas on each side over a gas flame or in a dry skillet until they are malleable.

7. To assemble the Cilantro Lime Shrimp Tacos, place a layer of shredded lettuce or cabbage on each warm tortilla.

8. Top the lettuce with a generous amount of Cilantro Lime Shrimp.

9. Add sliced avocado or guacamole, sliced red onion, and sliced jalapeño on top of the shrimp for additional flavors and textures.

10. Sprinkle more chopped fresh cilantro over the tacos for a burst of herbal freshness.

11. Serve the delectable Cilantro Lime Shrimp Tacos with lime wedges on the side for squeezing over the tacos.

12. Enjoy the zesty and succulent Cilantro Lime Shrimp Tacos as a mouthwatering and satisfying meal!

Nutritional Info Per Serving
(2 tacos, excluding optional items):

Calories: 330 | Fats: 11g | Carbs: 33g | Proteins: 25g | Potassium: 450mg | Sodium: 390mg

Baked Chicken and Sweet Potato Fries

⅞ *Prep time: 15 minutes*

🍲 *Cook time: 30 minutes*

🍽 *Servings: 4*

Ingredients:

- For the Baked Chicken:
- 4 boneless, skinless chicken breasts
- 2 tablespoons olive oil
- 1 teaspoon garlic powder
- 1 teaspoon paprika
- 1/2 teaspoon dried thyme
- 1/2 teaspoon dried rosemary
- Salt and pepper to taste
- For the Sweet Potato Fries:
- 2 large sweet potatoes, peeled and cut into matchsticks
- 2 tablespoons olive oil
- 1/2 teaspoon ground cumin
- 1/2 teaspoon smoked paprika
- Salt and pepper to taste
- Optional dipping sauce:
- Greek yogurt sprinkled with freshly chopped cilantro and a dash of lime

Directions:

1. Set the oven temperature to 425°F (220°C).

2. Combine olive oil, garlic powder, paprika, dried thyme, dried rosemary, salt, and pepper in a small bowl to make the chicken marinade.

3. Place the chicken breasts in a shallow dish or in a sealable plastic bag.

4. Cover each breast with the marinade by pouring it over the chicken. For even dispersion, massage the marinade into the chicken.

5. To enable the flavors to meld, cover the dish or seal the bag and place the chicken in the refrigerator for at least 15 minutes, preferably 1-2 hours.

6. Prepare the sweet potato fries while the chicken is marinating. Thoroughly coat the sweet potato matchsticks in a big bowl with olive oil, ground cumin, smoked paprika, salt, and pepper.

7. Place the sweet potato fries in a single layer on a baking sheet lined with parchment paper.

8. Bake the sweet potato fries in the preheated oven for 20 to 25 minutes, flipping them halfway through to ensure even cooking. Continue baking until the fries are crispy and lightly browned.

9. Get the chicken ready while the sweet potato fries are baking. Preheat a large, oven-safe skillet on medium-high.
10. Add the marinated chicken breasts to the hot skillet and cook them for a couple of minutes on each side, or until they have a golden crust.
11. In the preheated oven with the skillet containing the seared chicken, bake the chicken for 15 to 20 minutes, or until it is well done and the middle is no longer pink.
12. Once the chicken and sweet potato fries are done, remove them from the oven.
13. Optional: Serve the baked chicken and sweet potato fries with a Greek yogurt dipping sauce made by combining Greek yogurt, lime juice, and fresh cilantro.
14. Serve the delicious and healthy Baked Chicken and Sweet Potato Fries together for a satisfying and nourishing meal!

Nutritional Info Per Serving
(1/4 of the recipe, excluding optional items):

Calories: 350 | Fats: 15g | Carbs: 30g | Proteins: 28g | Potassium: 820mg | Sodium: 360mg

Tomato Basil Quinoa Salad

Prep time: 15 minutes
Cook time: 15 minutes
Servings: 4

Ingredients:
- 1 cup quinoa, rinsed
- 2 cups vegetable broth or water
- 1/4 cup crumbled feta cheese (optional, for serving)
- 1 cup cherry tomatoes, halved
- 1/4 cup chopped red onion
- 1/2 cup fresh basil leaves, thinly sliced
- 2 tablespoons extra-virgin olive oil
- 2 tablespoons balsamic vinegar
- 1 clove garlic, minced
- Salt and pepper to taste

Directions:
1. Combine the washed quinoa with water or vegetable broth in a saucepan. Over high heat, quickly bring the liquid to a boil. Once it starts to boil, lower the heat to low and simmer the quinoa for about 15 minutes, or until the liquid is absorbed and the quinoa is cooked.
2. While the quinoa is cooking, prepare the salad dressing. In a small bowl, add the extra virgin olive oil, balsamic vinegar, garlic powder, salt, and pepper to prepare the dressing.
3. Place the cooked quinoa, halved cherry tomatoes, thinly sliced fresh basil, and finely chopped red onion in a large mixing bowl.
4. Pour the dressing over the quinoa salad ingredients, and toss everything together until the dressing is well distributed.
5. Optional: Add crumbled feta cheese to the quinoa salad for extra creaminess and flavor.
6. If necessary, add extra salt and pepper after tasting the tomato-basil quinoa salad.
7. Divide the flavorful and colorful Tomato Basil Quinoa Salad into individual serving bowls or plates.
8. Serve the refreshing and nutrient-rich Tomato Basil Quinoa Salad as a delightful and wholesome side dish or a light and satisfying main course.

Nutritional Info Per Serving
(1/4 of the recipe, excluding optional item):

Calories: 240 | Fats: 12g | Carbs: 27g | Proteins: 7g | Potassium: 370mg | Sodium: 220mg

Turkey Meatball Lettuce Wraps

Prep time: 20 minutes

Cook time: 20 minutes

Servings: 4 lettuce wraps

Ingredients:

- For the Turkey Meatballs:
- 1 pound ground turkey
- 1/4 cup breadcrumbs (whole wheat or gluten-free, if desired)
- 1 large egg
- 1/4 cup grated Parmesan cheese
- 2 cloves garlic, minced
- 1 tablespoon chopped fresh parsley
- 1 teaspoon dried oregano
- 1/2 teaspoon onion powder
- Salt and pepper to taste
- For the Lettuce Wraps:
- 8 large lettuce leaves (such as iceberg, romaine, or butter lettuce)
- 1 cup diced tomatoes
- 1/2 cup diced cucumber
- 1/4 cup thinly sliced red onion
- 1/4 cup crumbled feta cheese (optional, for serving)
- Greek yogurt or tzatziki sauce (for serving)

Directions:

1. Set the oven temperature to 375°F (190°C).
2. Combine the ground turkey, breadcrumbs, egg, grated Parmesan cheese, dried oregano, onion powder, minced garlic, fresh parsley, and salt and pepper in a large mixing bowl.
3. Mix everything together until all the ingredients are well incorporated.
4. Make meatballs out of the turkey mixture that are about an inch in diameter using your hands.
5. Put the meatballs on a parchment paper-lined baking sheet.
6. Bake the turkey meatballs in the preheated oven for about 18-20 minutes or until they are cooked through and lightly browned.
7. While the meatballs are baking, prepare the lettuce wraps. Wash and pat dry the lettuce leaves.
8. In each lettuce leaf, place a few baked turkey meatballs.
9. Top the meatballs with diced tomatoes, diced cucumber, and thinly sliced red onion for added freshness and crunch.
10. Optional: Sprinkle crumbled feta cheese over the lettuce wraps for extra creaminess and flavor.
11. Drizzle Greek yogurt or tzatziki sauce over the Turkey Meatball Lettuce Wraps for a tangy and savory finish.
12. Fold the sides of the lettuce leaf over the filling, and then roll it up like a burrito to create the lettuce wraps.
13. Repeat the process with the remaining lettuce leaves and turkey meatballs to make a total of 4 lettuce wraps.
14. Serve the delectable and protein-packed Turkey Meatball Lettuce Wraps as a light and satisfying meal!

Nutritional Info Per Serving
(1 lettuce wrap, excluding optional items):

Calories: 250 | Fats: 13g | Carbs: 11g | Proteins: 23g | Potassium: 420mg | Sodium: 320mg

Eggplant and Chickpea Curry

Prep time: 15 minutes

Cook time: 30 minutes

Servings: 4

Ingredients:

- 1 large eggplant, diced
- 1 can (15 ounces) chickpeas,

drained and rinsed
- 1 onion, finely chopped
- 3 cloves garlic, minced
- 1 tablespoon fresh ginger, grated
- 1 can (14 ounces) diced tomatoes
- 1 can (13.5 ounces) coconut milk
- 2 tablespoons curry powder
- 1 teaspoon ground cumin
- 1/2 teaspoon ground turmeric
- 1/4 teaspoon cayenne pepper (optional, for heat)
- Salt and pepper to taste
- 2 tablespoons vegetable oil
- Fresh cilantro, for garnish
- Cooked rice or naan bread, for serving

⌧ Directions:

1. Heat the vegetable oil in a big skillet or pot over medium heat.
2. Place the chopped onion in the skillet and cook for 2 to 3 minutes, or until transparent.
3. When aromatic, add the grated ginger and minced garlic and simmer for an additional one to two minutes.
4. Stir in the chopped eggplant and simmer the mixture for 5 minutes, or until the eggplant begins to soften.
5. Sprinkle the curry powder, ground cumin, ground turmeric, cayenne pepper (if using), salt, and pepper over the eggplant mixture. Stir to coat the eggplant with the spices.
6. Pour in the diced tomatoes and drained chickpeas. Stir again to combine all the ingredients.
7. Lower the heat to medium-low, and let the eggplant and chickpea mixture simmer for about 15 minutes, allowing the flavors to meld together.
8. Add the coconut milk and boil the curry for an additional 10 minutes, or until the sauce slightly thickens.
9. Taste the curry made with eggplant and chickpeas, and season the

spices with more salt and pepper if necessary.
10. Optional: Garnish the curry with fresh cilantro for added herbal freshness.
11. For a rich and cozy lunch, serve the delicious Eggplant and Chickpea Curry over cooked rice or with warm naan bread.

Nutritional Info Per Serving
(excluding optional items and serving side):

Calories: 340 | Fats: 21g | Carbs: 31g | Proteins: 9g | Potassium: 670mg | Sodium: 450mg

Garlic Shrimp and Spinach Salad

⅛ *Prep time: 15 minutes*

🍲 *Cook time: 10 minutes*

🍽 *Servings: 4*

🍲 Ingredients:

- For the Garlic Shrimp:
- 1 pound large shrimp, peeled and deveined
- 4 cloves garlic, minced
- 2 tablespoons olive oil
- 1 teaspoon paprika
- 1/2 teaspoon red pepper flakes (optional, for heat)
- Salt and pepper to taste
- For the Spinach Salad:
- 6 cups fresh baby spinach leaves
- 1 cup cherry tomatoes, halved
- 1/4 cup sliced red onion
- 1/4 cup crumbled feta cheese (optional, for serving)
- Lemon wedges (for serving)
- For the Dressing:
- 2 tablespoons extra-virgin olive oil
- 2 tablespoons balsamic vinegar
- 1 teaspoon Dijon mustard
- 1 teaspoon honey or maple syrup (for a vegan option)
- Salt and pepper to taste

Directions:

1. In a medium bowl, combine the shrimp that have been peeled and deveined with the garlic powder, olive oil, paprika, red pepper flakes (if using), salt, and pepper. The shrimp should be coated completely after being tossed in the marinade with the garlic. Give the shrimp about 10 minutes to marinate while you prepare the rest of the salad ingredients.
2. Heat a large skillet to medium-high.
3. When the skillet is heated, add the marinated shrimp.
4. Cook the shrimp for about 2-3 minutes on each side or until they are pink and cooked through. Be careful not to overcook the shrimp to keep them tender and juicy.
5. While the shrimp are cooking, prepare the salad dressing. To create the dressing, combine the extra virgin olive oil, balsamic vinegar, Dijon mustard, honey or maple syrup (if using), salt, and pepper in a small bowl.
6. In a large salad bowl, combine the fresh baby spinach leaves, halved cherry tomatoes, and sliced red onion.
7. Pour the dressing over the spinach salad ingredients, and toss everything together until the salad is well coated with the dressing.
8. Divide the dressed spinach salad into individual serving plates or bowls.
9. Top each plate of spinach salad with the garlic shrimp.
10. Optional: Sprinkle crumbled feta cheese over the salad for extra creaminess and tanginess.
11. Place lemon wedges on the side for guests to squeeze over the tasty and healthy Garlic Shrimp and Spinach Salad.

12. For a tasty and filling supper, savor the delicious and protein-rich Garlic Shrimp and Spinach Salad!

Nutritional Info Per Serving
(1/4 of the recipe, excluding optional items):

Calories: 240 | Fats: 14g | Carbs: 11g | Proteins: 20g | Potassium: 620mg | Sodium: 370mg

Lemon Garlic Tilapia with Quinoa

Prep time: 10 minutes

Cook time: 20 minutes

Servings: 4

Ingredients:

- For the Lemon Garlic Tilapia:
- 4 tilapia fillets (about 4-6 ounces each)
- Zest of 1 lemon
- Juice of 2 lemons
- 4 cloves garlic, minced
- 2 tablespoons olive oil
- 1 teaspoon dried oregano
- Salt and pepper to taste
- For the Quinoa:
- 1 cup quinoa, rinsed
- 2 cups vegetable broth or water
- 1 tablespoon olive oil
- 1/4 cup chopped fresh parsley
- Salt and pepper to taste
- Optional Garnish:
- Lemon slices
- Fresh parsley leaves

Directions:

1. The lemon zest, lemon juice, minced garlic, olive oil, dried oregano, salt, and pepper are combined in a shallow dish to make the marinade for the tilapia.
2. Place the tilapia fillets in the marinade, making sure they are coated on both sides. Let the tilapia marinate for about 10 minutes while you prepare the quinoa.

3. Heat the rinsed quinoa in a saucepan with water or vegetable broth. Bring the liquid to a quick boil over high heat. Once it begins to boil, immediately reduce the heat to low and let the quinoa simmer for about 15 minutes, or until the liquid is absorbed and the quinoa is cooked.
4. Start heating a large skillet over medium-high heat while the quinoa is cooking.
5. Add the marinated tilapia fillets to the heated skillet. The tilapia should be cooked for 3 to 4 minutes on each side, or until they are completely done and easily flake with a fork.
6. Combine the cooked quinoa with the chopped fresh parsley, olive oil, salt, and pepper while the tilapia is cooking.
7. Optional: Garnish the quinoa with lemon slices and fresh parsley leaves for an appealing presentation.
8. Divide the Lemon Garlic Tilapia and Quinoa into individual serving plates or bowls.
9. Serve the flavorful and wholesome Lemon Garlic Tilapia with Quinoa for a light and nutritious meal!

Nutritional Info Per Serving
(1/4 of the recipe, excluding optional items):

Calories: 330 | Fats: 12g | Carbs: 24g | Proteins: 30g | Potassium: 520mg | Sodium: 260mg

Black Bean and Avocado Wrap

Prep time: 15 minutes
Cook time: 5 minutes
Servings: 4 wraps

Ingredients:
- 1 ripe avocado, pitted and sliced
- 1 cup diced tomatoes
- 1 can (15 ounces) black beans, drained and rinsed
- 1/4 cup diced red onion
- 1/4 cup chopped fresh cilantro
- Juice of 1 lime
- 1 teaspoon ground cumin
- Salt and pepper to taste
- 4 large whole wheat or spinach tortillas
- Optional Additions:
- Sliced bell peppers
- Shredded lettuce or cabbage
- Sliced jalapeño (for heat)
- Grated cheddar cheese
- Greek yogurt or sour cream (for serving)

Directions:
1. Combine the black beans, diced tomatoes, diced red onion, diced avocado, and fresh cilantro in a big bowl.
2. Sprinkle salt, pepper, and ground cumin over the mixture after squeezing the lime juice over it.
3. Gently toss everything together until the ingredients are well combined and coated with the lime-cumin dressing.
4. Briefly heat the tortillas on each side over a gas flame or in a dry skillet until they are soft and malleable.
5. Divide the black bean and avocado mixture evenly among the warm tortillas, placing the filling in the center of each tortilla.
6. Optional: Add sliced bell peppers, shredded lettuce or cabbage, sliced jalapeño, or grated cheddar cheese to the wraps for additional flavors and textures.
7. To make the wraps, fold the tortilla's sides over the contents and then close it securely.
8. Slice each wrap in half diagonally, if desired, for easier handling.
9. Serve the delectable and nutrient-rich Black Bean and Avocado Wraps with Greek yogurt or sour

cream on the side for dipping or drizzling.
10. Enjoy the delightful and protein-packed Black Bean and Avocado Wraps for a satisfying and flavorful meal!

Nutritional Info Per Serving
(1 wrap, excluding optional items):

Calories: 290 | Fats: 10g | Carbs: 40g | Proteins: 10g | Potassium: 580mg | Sodium: 490mg

Dinner Recipes

Lemon Herb Baked Salmon

🍴 *Prep time: 10 minutes*

🍲 *Cook time: 15 minutes*

🍽 *Servings: 4*

🥄 **Ingredients:**

- 4 salmon fillets (about 4-6 ounces each)
- Zest of 1 lemon
- Juice of 2 lemons
- 2 tablespoons olive oil
- 2 cloves garlic, minced
- 1 tablespoon chopped fresh parsley
- 1 tablespoon chopped fresh dill
- 1 teaspoon dried oregano
- Salt and pepper to taste
- Lemon slices (for garnish)
- Fresh dill sprigs (for garnish)

🔲 **Directions:**

1. Set the oven temperature to 400°F (200°C).
2. To make the salmon marinade, combine the lemon zest, lemon juice, olive oil, minced garlic, fresh parsley, fresh dill, dried oregano, salt, and pepper in a small bowl.
3. Put the salmon fillets in a sealable plastic bag or a shallow dish.
4. Pour the marinade over the salmon, making sure each fillet is coated with the herb-infused lemon marinade.
5. While the oven is heating up, cover the dish or close the bag and let the salmon marinate for about 10 minutes.
6. Line a baking sheet with parchment paper.
7. On the prepared baking sheet, arrange the salmon fillets that have been marinated in a single layer.
8. Optional: Place lemon slices on top of each salmon fillet for added lemony flavor.
9. Bake the salmon in the preheated oven for 12 to 15 minutes, or until it is thoroughly cooked and easily flakes with a fork.
10. After the salmon has finished roasting, take it out of the oven and give it a moment to rest.
11. Optional: Garnish the Lemon Herb Baked Salmon with fresh dill sprigs for an appealing presentation.
12. Divide the flavorful and nutritious Lemon Herb Baked Salmon into individual serving plates.
13. Serve the succulent and Omega-3-rich Lemon Herb Baked Salmon with your choice of healthy sides, such as steamed vegetables, quinoa, or a green salad, for a wholesome and satisfying dinner!

Nutritional Info Per Serving
(1 salmon fillet, excluding optional items):

Calories: 300 | Fats: 18g | Carbs: 2g | Proteins: 32g | Potassium: 680mg | Sodium: 160mg

Quinoa-Stuffed Bell Peppers

🍴 *Prep time: 20 minutes*

🍲 *Cook time: 40 minutes*

🍽 *Servings: 4 stuffed bell peppers*

🥄 **Ingredients:**

- 4 large bell peppers (any color), tops cut off and seeds removed
- 1 cup quinoa, rinsed
- 2 cups vegetable broth or water
- 1 tablespoon olive oil
- 1 small onion, finely chopped
- 2 cloves garlic, minced
- 1 cup diced tomatoes

(canned or fresh)
- 1 cup cooked black beans (canned or cooked from dry)
- 1 teaspoon ground cumin
- 1/2 teaspoon smoked paprika
- 1/4 teaspoon chili powder (optional, for heat)
- Salt and pepper to taste
- 1/2 cup grated cheddar or mozzarella cheese (optional, for topping)
- Fresh cilantro or parsley, for garnish

☒ **Directions:**

1. Set the oven temperature to 375°F (190°C).
2. Combine the rinsed quinoa with water or vegetable broth in a saucepan. Over high heat, quickly bring the liquid to a boil. Simmer the quinoa for about 15 minutes, or until all the liquid is absorbed and the quinoa is cooked, on low heat with the lid on the pan.
3. Heat olive oil in a large skillet over medium heat while the quinoa is boiling.
4. Add the chopped onion to the skillet and cook for 3 to 4 minutes, or until translucent.
5. Stir in the minced garlic, diced tomatoes, and cooked black beans. Cook everything together for another 2-3 minutes.
6. Season the mixture with ground cumin, smoked paprika, chili powder (if using), salt, and pepper. Stir to combine all the flavors.
7. Once the quinoa is cooked, add it to the skillet with the onion, garlic, tomatoes, and black beans. Mix everything together until the quinoa is well incorporated with the other ingredients.
8. Gently push the quinoa mixture into each bell pepper to ensure that it is evenly distributed.
9. Set the peppers that have been filled in a baking dish.

10. Optional: Sprinkle grated cheddar or mozzarella cheese over the top of each stuffed bell pepper for extra creaminess and flavor.
11. Cover the baking dish with aluminum foil.
12. Once the oven is warmed, bake the quinoa-stuffed bell peppers for 25 to 30 minutes, or until the peppers are soft and the filling is thoroughly cooked.
13. Remove the lid and bake the dish for an additional 5 to 10 minutes to melt the cheese and turn it golden brown.
14. Once the stuffed bell peppers are done baking, remove them from the oven and let them cool slightly.
15. To add some color and herbal freshness, garnish the quinoa-stuffed bell peppers with fresh cilantro or parsley.
16. Serve the flavorful and nutrient-rich Quinoa-Stuffed Bell Peppers as a wholesome and delightful meal!

Nutritional Info Per Serving
(1 stuffed bell pepper, excluding optional items):

Calories: 310 | Fats: 8g | Carbs: 48g | Proteins: 14g | Potassium: 780mg | Sodium: 530mg

Moroccan Chickpea Stew

🎚 *Prep time: 15 minutes*

🍲 *Cook time: 30 minutes*

🍽 *Servings: 4*

🥄 **Ingredients:**

- 1 tablespoon olive oil
- 1 onion, finely chopped
- 3 cloves garlic, minced
- 1 red bell pepper, diced
- 2 carrots, peeled and diced
- 1 teaspoon ground cumin
- 1 teaspoon ground coriander
- 1/2 teaspoon ground cinnamon
- 1/2 teaspoon ground ginger
- 1/4 teaspoon cayenne pepper (optional, for heat)

- 1 can (14 ounces) diced tomatoes
- 2 cups vegetable broth
- 2 cans (15 ounces each) chickpeas, drained and rinsed
- 1 cup chopped butternut squash
- 1/4 cup chopped dried apricots
- 1/4 cup chopped fresh cilantro
- Salt and pepper to taste
- Optional Garnish:
- Fresh cilantro leaves
- Toasted almond slices

⌧ Directions:

1. Use a large pot or Dutch to heat the olive oil over medium heat.
2. Add the finely chopped onion to the pot, and sauté it for about 3-4 minutes until it becomes translucent.
3. Stir in the minced garlic, diced red bell pepper, and diced carrots. Cook everything together for another 2-3 minutes until the vegetables begin to soften.
4. Add the ground cumin, ground coriander, ground cinnamon, ground ginger, and cayenne pepper (if using) to the pot. Stir to coat the vegetables with the aromatic spices.
5. Add the vegetable broth and diced tomatoes. Simmer.
6. Add the drained and rinsed chickpeas, chopped butternut squash, and chopped dried apricots to the pot. Stir to combine all the ingredients.
7. Simmer the Moroccan Chickpea Stew with the lid on and the heat set to low for 20 to 25 minutes, or until the butternut squash is cooked and the flavors are harmonious.
8. Once you've tasted the stew, season it with salt and pepper to your liking.
9. Stir in the chopped fresh cilantro to add a burst of herbal freshness to the stew.
10. Optional: Garnish the Moroccan Chickpea Stew with fresh cilantro

leaves and toasted almond slices for added visual appeal and crunch.
11. Serve the flavorful and protein-rich Moroccan Chickpea Stew as a comforting and satisfying dinner!

Nutritional Info Per Serving
(1/4 of the recipe, excluding optional items):

Calories: 350 | Fats: 7g | Carbs: 61g | Proteins: 15g | Potassium: 950mg | Sodium: 550mg

Garlic Shrimp and Broccoli Stir-fry

🥄 *Prep time: 10 minutes*
🍳 *Cook time: 15 minutes*
🍽 *Servings: 4*

⌧ Ingredients:

- 1 pound large shrimp, peeled and deveined
- 2 cups broccoli florets
- 1 red bell pepper, thinly sliced
- 2 cloves garlic, minced
- 1 tablespoon grated fresh ginger
- 3 tablespoons soy sauce (low-sodium)
- 1 tablespoon oyster sauce (optional, for added umami flavor)
- 1 tablespoon sesame oil
- 1 tablespoon vegetable oil
- 1 teaspoon cornstarch (or arrowroot powder)
- 1/4 cup water or vegetable broth
- 1 tablespoon sesame seeds (for garnish)
- Sliced green onions (for garnish)
- Cooked brown rice or quinoa (for serving)

⌧ Directions:

1. To make the stir-fry sauce, combine the soy sauce, oyster sauce (if using), sesame oil, cornstarch, and vegetable or water broth in a small bowl. Set aside.

2. In a wok or big skillet, heat the vegetable oil over medium-high heat.
3. Add the freshly grated ginger and garlic powder to the wok. Stir-fry for around 30 seconds or until they start to smell good.
4. After adding the shrimp, stir-fry them for 2–3 minutes, or until they become pink and are fully cooked. Place the cooked shrimp on a platter.
5. In the same wok, add the broccoli florets and sliced red bell pepper. Stir-fry the vegetables for about 3-4 minutes until they are tender-crisp.
6. Return the cooked shrimp to the wok with the vegetables.
7. Pour the stir-fry sauce over the shrimp and vegetables. Toss everything together to coat the ingredients evenly with the savory sauce.
8. Stir-fry with broccoli and garlic shrimp should be cooked for an extra one to two minutes to allow the sauce to slightly thicken.
9. Optional: Sprinkle sesame seeds over the stir-fry for added crunch and nutty flavor.
10. Remove the wok from the heat.
11. Optional: Sliced green onions can be used as a garnish to the Garlic Shrimp and Broccoli Stir-Fry to add color and freshness.
12. Serve the delectable and protein-packed Garlic Shrimp and Broccoli Stir-fry over cooked brown rice or quinoa for a satisfying and healthy dinner!

Nutritional Info Per Serving
(1/4 of the recipe, excluding optional items and serving side):

Calories: 280 | Fats: 10g | Carbs: 15g | Proteins: 30g | Potassium: 520mg | Sodium: 700mg

Greek Chicken Souvlaki Skewers

Prep time: 20 minutes

Marinating time: 1 hour (or overnight)

Cook time: 10 minutes

Servings: 4 skewers

Ingredients:

- *For* the Chicken Souvlaki:
- 1 pound boneless, skinless chicken breasts or thighs, cut into 1-inch cubes
- 1/4 cup olive oil
- 2 tablespoons lemon juice
- 2 cloves garlic, minced
- 1 teaspoon dried oregano
- 1 teaspoon dried thyme
- 1 teaspoon dried rosemary
- 1/2 teaspoon ground cumin
- Salt and pepper to taste
- For the Tzatziki Sauce:
- 1 cup Greek yogurt
- 1/2 cucumber, grated and squeezed to remove excess water
- 1 clove garlic, minced
- 1 tablespoon lemon juice
- 1 tablespoon chopped fresh dill
- Salt and pepper to taste
- For Serving:
- 4 pita bread or flatbreads
- Sliced red onion
- Sliced tomatoes
- Sliced cucumber
- Fresh parsley, for garnish

Directions:

1. To make the marinade for the chicken souvlaki, combine the olive oil, lemon juice, minced garlic, dried oregano, dried thyme, dried rosemary, powdered cumin, salt, and pepper in a bowl.
2. Cut chicken into cubes and add it to the marinade. Toss to evenly distribute the flavorful mixture over the meat.

3. Place plastic wrap over the bowl or place the chicken and marinade in a zip-top bag. For the finest flavor, let the chicken marinate in the refrigerator for at least an hour (or overnight).
4. Make the tzatziki sauce while the chicken marinates. Combine Greek yogurt, grated cucumber, minced garlic, lemon juice, chopped fresh dill, salt, and pepper in a small bowl. Place the sauce in the fridge before serving.
5. Turn the heat to medium-high and preheat your grill or grill pan.
6. Skewer the marinated chicken cubes. Make sure to soak wooden skewers in water for around 20 minutes before use to avoid scorching them.
7. Grill the Chicken Souvlaki Skewers for about 4-5 minutes on each side or until the chicken is cooked through and has a nice char.
8. While the chicken is grilling, warm the pita bread or flatbreads on the grill for a few seconds on each side.
9. Remove the Chicken Souvlaki Skewers from the grill, and let them rest for a minute.
10. To serve, spread some tzatziki sauce on each warmed pita bread or flatbread.
11. Place a Chicken Souvlaki Skewer on top of the sauce.
12. Add sliced red onion, sliced tomatoes, and sliced cucumber over the chicken.
13. Optional: Garnish the Chicken Souvlaki Skewers with fresh parsley for added herbal freshness.
14. Fold the pita bread or flatbread over the toppings, creating a wrap or sandwich.
15. Serve the mouthwatering Greek Chicken Souvlaki Skewers with Tzatziki Sauce for a delicious and authentic Mediterranean-inspired meal!

Nutritional Info Per Serving
(1 skewer with pita and toppings, excluding optional items):
Calories: 390 | Fats: 16g | Carbs: 27g | Proteins: 32g | Potassium: 490mg | Sodium: 400mg

Vegetable Lentil Curry

Prep time: 15 minutes
Cook time: 30 minutes
Servings: 4

Ingredients:

- 1 cup dry green or brown lentils, rinsed
- 1 tablespoon vegetable oil
- 1 onion, finely chopped
- 3 cloves garlic, minced
- 1 tablespoon grated fresh ginger
- 1 red bell pepper, diced
- 1 zucchini, diced
- 1 carrot, diced
- 1 cup diced tomatoes (canned or fresh)
- 1 can (13.5 ounces) coconut milk
- 2 tablespoons curry powder
- 1 teaspoon ground cumin
- 1/2 teaspoon ground coriander
- 1/4 teaspoon cayenne pepper (optional, for heat)
- Salt and pepper to taste
- Fresh cilantro, for garnish
- Cooked brown rice or naan bread (for serving)

Directions:

1. In a saucepan, combine the rinsed lentils with 2 cups of water. Briskly bring the mixture to a boil over medium-high heat. Turn the heat down to low after it begins to boil, cover the pan, and allow the lentils to simmer for 15 to 20 minutes, or until they are tender. Drain any excess water after the lentils have finished cooking, then set them aside.

2. Over medium heat, warm the vegetable oil in a big skillet or Dutch oven.
3. Add the finely chopped onion to the skillet, and sauté it for about 3-4 minutes until it becomes translucent.
4. Stir in the minced garlic and grated fresh ginger. Cook everything together for another 1-2 minutes until they become fragrant.
5. Add the diced red bell pepper, diced zucchini, and diced carrot to the skillet. Stir-fry the vegetables for about 3-4 minutes until they start to soften.
6. Add the coconut milk and diced tomatoes. Combine all of the ingredients.
7. Season the curry with curry powder, ground cumin, ground coriander, cayenne pepper (if using), salt, and pepper. Stir to combine all the flavors.
8. Add the cooked lentils to the skillet, and mix everything together until the lentils are well incorporated with the vegetables and the creamy curry sauce.
9. Let the Vegetable Lentil Curry simmer for an additional 5-10 minutes over low heat to allow the flavors to meld together.
10. Optional: Garnish the curry with fresh cilantro for a pop of color and herbal freshness.
11. Serve the delectable and protein-packed Vegetable Lentil Curry with cooked brown rice or naan bread for a comforting and nutritious dinner!

Nutritional Info Per Serving
(1/4 of the recipe, excluding optional items and serving side):

Calories: 390 | Fats: 23g | Carbs: 37g | Proteins: 13g| Potassium: 890mg | Sodium: 450mg

Balsamic Glazed Chicken Thighs

Prep time: 10 minutes

Marinating time: 30 minutes (or overnight)

Cook time: 25 minutes

Servings: 4

Ingredients:

- 8 bone-in, skin-on chicken thighs
- 1/4 cup balsamic vinegar
- 2 tablespoons olive oil
- 2 tablespoons honey
- 3 cloves garlic, minced
- 1 teaspoon dried thyme
- 1/2 teaspoon dried rosemary
- 1/2 teaspoon dried oregano
- Salt and pepper to taste
- Fresh thyme sprigs (for garnish)
- Lemon wedges (for serving)

Directions:

1. To make the marinade for the chicken thighs, combine the balsamic vinegar, olive oil, honey, minced garlic, dried thyme, dried rosemary, dried oregano, salt, and pepper in a bowl.
2. Put the chicken thighs in a large shallow dish or resealable plastic bag.
3. Pour the balsamic glaze marinade over the chicken thighs, making sure each piece is coated with the flavorful mixture.
4. For the best flavor, marinate the chicken thighs in the fridge for at least 30 minutes (or overnight) with the bag or dish covered.
5. Set the oven temperature to 425°F (220°C).
6. Remove the marinated chicken thighs from the refrigerator and let them sit at room temperature for a few minutes.

7. Place the chicken thighs skin side up on a baking sheet covered with parchment paper.
8. Brush some of the remaining marinade over the top of each chicken thigh.
9. Bake the Balsamic Glazed Chicken Thighs in the preheated oven for about 20-25 minutes or until the chicken is cooked through and the skin is golden and crispy.
10. While the chicken is baking, you can baste the thighs with more of the glaze midway through cooking for extra flavor and moisture.
11. Once the chicken thighs are done baking, remove them from the oven and let them rest for a few minutes.
12. Optional: Garnish the Balsamic Glazed Chicken Thighs with fresh thyme sprigs for added herbal fragrance.
13. Serve the succulent and flavorful Balsamic Glazed Chicken Thighs with lemon wedges on the side for a zesty touch!
14. Pair the Balsamic Glazed Chicken Thighs with your choice of healthy sides, such as roasted vegetables, quinoa, or a green salad, for a wholesome and delightful dinner!

Nutritional Info Per Serving
(2 chicken thighs, excluding optional items and serving side):
Calories: 480 | Fats: 28g | Carbs: 19g | Proteins: 37g | Potassium: 480mg | Sodium: 220mg

Asian Turkey Lettuce Wraps

Prep time: 15 minutes
Cook time: 15 minutes
Servings: 4

Ingredients:

- 1 pound ground turkey
- 1 tablespoon vegetable oil
- 1 onion, finely chopped
- 2 cloves garlic, minced
- 1 red bell pepper, diced
- 1 carrot, grated
- 1/4 cup hoisin sauce
- 2 tablespoons soy sauce (low-sodium)
- 1 tablespoon rice vinegar
- 1 tablespoon grated fresh ginger
- 1 teaspoon sesame oil
- 1/4 teaspoon red pepper flakes (optional, for heat)
- Salt and pepper to taste
- 1 head butter lettuce or iceberg lettuce
- Sliced green onions (for garnish)
- Sesame seeds (for garnish)

Directions:

1. In a large skillet, heat vegetable oil to a medium-high temperature.
2. Add the finely chopped onion to the skillet, and sauté it for about 3-4 minutes until it becomes translucent.
3. Stir in the minced garlic and grated fresh ginger. Cook everything together for another 1-2 minutes until fragrant.
4. When the ground turkey is fully cooked and no longer pink, add it to the skillet and heat it, breaking it up with a spatula as it cooks.
5. Add the grated carrot and diced red bell pepper. The vegetables should start to soften after 3 to 4 minutes of cooking everything together.
6. To make the sauce for the turkey filling, combine the hoisin sauce, soy sauce, rice vinegar, sesame oil, red pepper flakes (if using), salt, and pepper in a small dish.
7. Cover the turkey and vegetables in the skillet with the sauce. Stir everything together until the flavorful and fragrant sauce is evenly distributed over the turkey and vegetables.
8. To enable the flavors to mingle, simmer the Asian turkey

combination for an additional 2 to 3 minutes.

9. Optional: Garnish the Asian Turkey Lettuce Wraps with sliced green onions and sesame seeds for added visual appeal and nutty flavor.

10. Separate the leaves of the butter lettuce or iceberg lettuce to create cups for the turkey filling.

11. To serve, spoon the flavorful Asian Turkey mixture into each lettuce cup.

12. Enjoy the delectable and protein-packed Asian Turkey Lettuce Wraps as a wholesome and satisfying dinner!

Nutritional Info Per Serving
(1/4 of the recipe, excluding optional items):

Calories: 280 | Fats: 14g | Carbs: 17g| Proteins: 24g | Potassium: 520mg | Sodium: 470mg

Cauliflower Rice and Black Bean Bowl

※ *Prep time: 10 minutes*

🍲 *Cook time: 15 minutes*

🍽 *Servings: 4*

Ingredients:

- 1 medium head of cauliflower, riced (about 4 cups)
- 1 tablespoon olive oil
- 1 onion, finely chopped
- 2 cloves garlic, minced
- 1 red bell pepper, diced
- 1 can (15 ounces) black beans, drained and rinsed
- 1 cup corn kernels (fresh, frozen, or canned)
- 1 teaspoon ground cumin
- 1/2 teaspoon chili powder
- 1/4 teaspoon smoked paprika
- Salt and pepper to taste
- Fresh cilantro, for garnish
- Lime wedges, for serving

Directions:

1. Remove the leaves and the abrasive core from the cauliflower head before you begin to rice it. It should be divided into florets, then put in a food processor. The cauliflower should be pulsed until it resembles grains of rice. If you don't have a food processor, you may simply grate the cauliflower using a box grater.

2. In a large skillet or a wok, heat the olive oil over medium heat.

3. Add the finely chopped onion to the skillet, and sauté it for about 3-4 minutes until it becomes translucent.

4. Stir in the minced garlic and diced red bell pepper. Cook everything together for another 2-3 minutes until the pepper starts to soften.

5. Add the riced cauliflower to the skillet. Cook it for about 5-6 minutes until it becomes tender, stirring occasionally.

6. Add the black beans and corn kernels after mixing. To fully reheat the beans and corn, cook everything together for an additional 2 to 3 minutes.

7. Season the Cauliflower Rice and Black Bean Bowl with ground cumin, chili powder, smoked paprika, salt, and pepper. Mix all the ingredients together until the flavors are well combined.

8. Cook for another 1-2 minutes to allow the flavors to meld together.

9. Optional: Garnish the Cauliflower Rice and Black Bean Bowl with fresh cilantro for added herbal freshness.

10. Serve the delectable and nutrient-rich Cauliflower Rice and Black Bean Bowl with lime wedges on the side for a zesty touch!

11. Enjoy the wholesome and flavorful Cauliflower Rice and Black Bean Bowl as a satisfying and nourishing meal!

Teriyaki Tofu Stir-fry

Prep time: 20 minutes

Cook time: 15 minutes

Servings: 4

Ingredients:

- 14 ounces (400g) firm tofu, drained and cut into cubes
- 2 tablespoons vegetable oil
- 1 red bell pepper, thinly sliced
- 1 yellow bell pepper, thinly sliced
- 1 cup broccoli florets
- 1 cup snap peas
- 1/2 cup sliced carrots
- 3 cloves garlic, minced
- 1 tablespoon grated fresh ginger
- 1/4 cup low-sodium soy sauce (or tamari for a gluten-free option)
- 2 tablespoons mirin (or rice vinegar)
- 2 tablespoons honey (or maple syrup for a vegan option)
- 1 tablespoon cornstarch (or arrowroot powder)
- 1/4 cup water or vegetable broth
- Sesame seeds (for garnish)
- Sliced green onions (for garnish)
- Cooked brown rice or quinoa (for serving)

Directions:

1. Start by cutting the tofu into bite-sized chunks after patting it dry with paper towels.
2. Heat 1 tablespoon of vegetable oil to medium-high heat in a large skillet or wok.
3. Place the tofu cubes in the skillet and cook for 5–6 minutes, flipping them over halfway through, or until they are crisp and golden brown all over. Turn the tofu cubes lightly to achieve even cooking. Transfer the cooked tofu to a plate and set it aside.
4. Fill the same skillet with the last tablespoon of vegetable oil.
5. Stir in the minced garlic and grated fresh ginger. Cook everything together for about 1-2 minutes until they become fragrant.
6. Snap peas, red and yellow bell pepper slices, carrot slices, broccoli florets, and snap peas should all be added to the skillet. For 3 to 4 minutes, or until they start to soften, stir-fry the vegetables.
7. In a small bowl, mix the low-sodium soy sauce, mirin, honey (or maple syrup), cornstarch (or arrowroot powder), and water or vegetable broth to create the teriyaki sauce.
8. Pour the teriyaki sauce over the stir-fried vegetables in the skillet. Stir everything together until the vegetables are coated with the savory sauce.
9. Add the cooked tofu cubes back to the skillet. Toss them with the vegetables and sauce to combine everything.
10. Let the Teriyaki Tofu Stir-fry cook for an additional 1-2 minutes to heat everything through and thicken the sauce slightly.
11. Optional: Garnish the Teriyaki Tofu Stir-fry with sesame seeds and sliced green onions for added visual appeal and nutty flavor.
12. Serve the delightful and protein-packed Teriyaki Tofu Stir-fry over cooked brown rice or quinoa for a wholesome and flavorful meal!

Lemon Garlic Roasted Chicken

% *Prep time: 10 minutes*

Marinating time: 2 hours (or overnight)

Cook time: 1 hour

Servings: 4

Ingredients:

- 1 whole chicken (about 4 pounds)
- 1 lemon, juiced and zest
- 4 cloves garlic, minced
- 2 tablespoons olive oil
- 1 tablespoon chopped fresh rosemary (or 1 teaspoon dried rosemary)
- 1 tablespoon chopped fresh thyme (or 1 teaspoon dried thyme)
- 1 tablespoon chopped fresh parsley
- Salt and pepper to taste
- 1/2 cup low-sodium chicken broth

Directions:

1. To prepare the Lemon Garlic Roasted Chicken, start by rinsing the chicken thoroughly inside and out under cold running water. Pat it dry with paper towels.
2. Lemon juice, lemon zest, garlic, olive oil, rosemary, thyme, and parsley should all be combined in a small bowl to form the marinade. Add salt and pepper to taste.
3. Rub the marinade all over the chicken, including under the skin and inside the cavity. Make sure the chicken is well coated with the flavorful mixture.
4. Cover the chicken with plastic wrap or transfer it to a large resealable plastic bag. Let the chicken marinate in the refrigerator for at least 2 hours (or overnight) for the best taste.
5. Set the oven temperature to 425°F (220°C).
6. Arrange the marinated chicken breast up in a roasting pan or baking dish.
7. Add chicken broth to the roasting pan's bottom to keep the chicken moist as it roasts.
8. In a preheated oven, roast the lemon-garlic chicken for about an hour or until the thickest part of the thigh registers 165°F (74°C) on a meat thermometer.
9. To keep the chicken moist and tasty, baste it with the juices from the bottom of the roasting pan every 20 to 30 minutes.
10. Remove the chicken from the oven when it is thoroughly cooked and gorgeously golden, and let it rest for about 10 minutes before cutting.
11. Carve the lemon garlic roasted chicken, then plate the flavorful pieces.
12. To give the chicken pieces more flavor and moisture, drizzle some of the pan juices over them.
13. Optional: Garnish the Lemon Garlic Roasted Chicken with fresh rosemary and thyme sprigs for added visual appeal.
14. Serve the delightful and protein-rich Lemon Garlic Roasted Chicken with your choice of healthy sides, such as roasted vegetables or a green salad, for a wholesome and savory dinner!

Nutritional Info Per Serving

(1/4 of the chicken, excluding optional items and serving side):

Calories: 460 | Fats: 30g | Carbs: 1g | Proteins: 43g | Potassium: 490mg | Sodium: 210mg

Spicy Cajun Shrimp and Quinoa

Prep time: 10 minutes

Cook time: 20 minutes

Servings: 4

Ingredients:

- 1 cup quinoa, rinsed
- 1 pound large shrimp, peeled and deveined
- 2 tablespoons olive oil
- 1 tablespoon Cajun seasoning
- 1/2 teaspoon garlic powder
- 1/2 teaspoon onion powder
- 1/4 teaspoon smoked paprika
- 1/4 teaspoon cayenne pepper (adjust to desired spiciness)
- Salt and pepper to taste
- 1 red bell pepper, diced
1 yellow bell pepper, diced
- 1 cup cherry tomatoes, halved
- 3 green onions, thinly sliced
- Fresh parsley, for garnish
- Lemon wedges, for serving

Directions:

1. Bring two cups of water to a roaring boil in a medium saucepan. Add a dash of salt and the rinsed quinoa. Simmer the quinoa on low heat with the pan lid on for about 15 minutes, or until it is cooked and the water has been absorbed. With a fork, fluff the quinoa, then set it aside.
2. In a large bowl, toss the peeled and deveined shrimp with 1 tablespoon of olive oil, Cajun seasoning, garlic powder, onion powder, smoked paprika, cayenne pepper, salt, and pepper. Make sure the shrimp are evenly coated with the flavorful spice mix.
3. In a big skillet, heat the last tablespoon of olive oil over medium-high heat.
4. Add the seasoned shrimp to the skillet. Cook them for about 2-3

minutes per side until they are pink and cooked through. Be careful not to overcook the shrimp.
5. Remove the cooked shrimp from the skillet and set them aside
6. Add the diced red and yellow bell peppers to the same skillet. Sauté them for about 2-3 minutes until they start to soften.
7. Stir in the halved cherry tomatoes and sliced green onions. Cook everything together for another 1-2 minutes until the tomatoes are slightly softened.
8. Add the cooked quinoa to the skillet with the vegetables. Mix everything until the quinoa is well combined with the colorful veggies.
9. Gently fold the cooked Cajun shrimp into the quinoa mixture.
10. Let the Spicy Cajun Shrimp and Quinoa cook for 1-2 more minutes to heat everything through.
11. Optional: Garnish the dish with fresh parsley for added herbal fragrance.
12. Serve the delightful and protein-packed Spicy Cajun Shrimp and Quinoa with lemon wedges on the side for a zesty touch!
13. Enjoy this flavorful and wholesome dish as a delightful and balanced meal!

Nutritional Info Per Serving
(1/4 of the recipe, excluding optional items and serving side):

Calories: 380 | Fats: 11g | Carbs: 40g | Proteins: 30g | Potassium: 730mg | Sodium: 450mg

Grilled Portobello Mushroom Steaks

Prep time: 15 minutes

Marinating time: 30 minutes (or longer for more flavor)

Cook time: 10 minutes

Servings: 4

Ingredients:

- 4 large portobello mushrooms, stems removed
- 3 tablespoons balsamic vinegar
- 2 tablespoons olive oil
- 2 cloves garlic, minced
- 1 teaspoon dried thyme
- 1 teaspoon dried rosemary
- 1/2 teaspoon smoked paprika
- Salt and pepper to taste
- Fresh parsley, for garnish
- Balsamic glaze (optional, for serving)

Directions:

1. Make the marinade in a shallow dish by combining the balsamic vinegar, olive oil, minced garlic, dried thyme, dried rosemary, smoked paprika, salt, and pepper.
2. Place the cleaned portobello mushrooms in the marinade, and use a brush or spoon to coat them thoroughly with the flavorful mixture. You can also make a few shallow cuts on the top side of the mushrooms to allow the marinade to penetrate better.
3. Use plastic wrap to seal the dish or place the mushrooms in a large resealable plastic bag. Marinate the mushrooms in the refrigerator for at least 30 minutes (or more for a stronger taste).
4. Set the temperature of your grill or grill pan to medium-high.
5. The grill grates or a grill pan should be lightly oiled with olive oil to prevent sticking.
6. Place the marinated portobello mushrooms on the grill, top side down. Reserve the leftover marinade for basting.
7. Grill the portobello mushrooms for about 4-5 minutes per side, or until they are tender and nicely charred, basting them with the reserved marinade occasionally.
8. Take the grilled portobello mushroom steaks from the grill when they are cooked to the level of doneness you choose, and give them a moment to rest.
9. Optional: Garnish the mushroom steaks with fresh parsley for added herbal fragrance.
10. Serve the delectable and meaty Grilled Portobello Mushroom Steaks with a drizzle of balsamic glaze on top for a touch of sweetness and acidity.
11. Enjoy these hearty and flavorful mushroom steaks as a delightful and nutritious meal!

Nutritional Info Per Serving
(1 mushroom steak, excluding optional items):

Calories: 90 | Fats: 7g | Carbs: 6g | Proteins: 3g | Potassium: 370mg | Sodium: 10mg

Blackened Tilapia with Mango Salsa

Prep time: 15 minutes

Cook time: 10 minutes

Servings: 4

Ingredients:

- *For* the Blackened Tilapia:
- 4 tilapia fillets (about 6 ounces each)
- 2 tablespoons olive oil
- 1 tablespoon smoked paprika
- 1 teaspoon ground cumin
- 1 teaspoon garlic powder
- 1/2 teaspoon onion powder
- 1/2 teaspoon cayenne pepper (adjust to desired spiciness)
- Salt and pepper to taste
- For the Mango Salsa:
- 2 ripe mangoes, peeled, pitted, and diced
- 1/2 red bell pepper, diced
- 1/4 cup finely chopped red onion
- 1 jalapeño, seeds removed and finely chopped
- 2 tablespoons fresh lime juice

- 2 tablespoons chopped fresh cilantro
- Salt and pepper to taste
- For serving:
- Cooked brown rice or quinoa
- Lime wedges

⌧ Directions:

1. For the Mango Salsa:
2. The diced mangoes, red bell pepper, finely chopped red onion, finely chopped jalapeño, fresh lime juice, finely chopped fresh cilantro, salt, and pepper are combined in a medium bowl to create the mango salsa.
3. Mix all the ingredients together until the flavors are well combined.
4. While you make the blackened tilapia, cover the bowl with plastic wrap and refrigerate the salsa.
5. For the Blackened Tilapia:
6. To make the blackening spice rub, combine the smoked paprika, ground cumin, garlic powder, onion powder, cayenne pepper, salt, and pepper in a small bowl.
7. After using paper towels to dry the tilapia fillets, massage each fillet with olive oil.
8. Generously coat each tilapia fillet with the blackening spice rub, pressing it onto the fish to adhere.
9. Heat a large skillet or grill pan to a high temperature.
10. Place the blackened tilapia fillets in the heated skillet and cook them for 3 to 4 minutes on each side, or until they are opaque throughout and have a blackened exterior.
11. Remove the cooked Blackened Tilapia from the skillet and let them rest for a minute.
12. For serving:
13. Serve the Blackened Tilapia on a bed of cooked brown rice or quinoa.
14. Top each tilapia fillet with a generous spoonful of the refreshing Mango Salsa.

15. Garnish the dish with fresh cilantro and lime wedges for added visual appeal and zesty flavor.
16. Enjoy this delectable and nutritious Blackened Tilapia with Mango Salsa for a delightful and balanced meal!

Nutritional Info Per Serving
(1 tilapia fillet with mango salsa, excluding optional items and serving side):

Calories: 290 | Fats: 11g | Carbs: 27g | Proteins: 23g | Potassium: 750mg | Sodium: 230mg

Caprese Chicken Salad

🍴 *Prep time: 15 minutes*

🍲 *Cook time: 20 minutes*

🥄 *Servings: 4*

⌁ Ingredients:

- 4 boneless, skinless chicken breasts
- 2 tablespoons balsamic vinegar
- 2 tablespoons olive oil
- 2 cloves garlic, minced
- 1 teaspoon dried basil
- Salt and pepper to taste
- 2 cups cherry tomatoes, halved
- 8 ounces fresh mozzarella, diced
- 1/4 cup fresh basil leaves, torn
- Balsamic glaze (optional, for drizzling)

⌧ Directions:

1. Prepare the marinade by combining the balsamic vinegar, olive oil, minced garlic, dried basil, salt, and pepper in a shallow dish.
2. Place the chicken breasts in the marinade, and use a brush or spoon to coat them thoroughly with the flavorful mixture.
3. Place plastic wrap over the serving dish or put the chicken and marinade in a large plastic bag that can be sealed. Let the chicken marinate in the refrigerator for at

least 30 minutes (or more for extra flavor).

4. Set the temperature of your grill or grill pan to medium-high.
5. Lightly oil the grill grates or grill pan with olive oil to prevent sticking.
6. Take the chicken out of the marinade and grill it for 5 to 6 minutes on each side, or until it is cooked through and has lovely grill marks. A meat thermometer should read 165°F (74°C) when the internal temperature is checked.
7. After the chicken has finished cooking, take it off the grill and give it a moment to rest before slicing.
8. To make the Caprese salad, add the diced fresh mozzarella, torn fresh basil leaves, and half cherry tomatoes in a large bowl.
9. Drizzle a little balsamic glaze over the salad ingredients for added sweetness and acidity (optional).
10. Cut the grilled chicken breasts into thin pieces.
11. Add the sliced grilled chicken to the Caprese salad, and gently toss everything together.
12. For an additional flavor boost, you can drizzle a bit more balsamic glaze over the finished Caprese Chicken Salad.
13. Serve the delightful and protein-packed Caprese Chicken Salad as a wholesome and satisfying meal!

Nutritional Info Per Serving
(1/4 of the recipe, excluding optional items):

Calories: 340 | Fats: 18g | Carbs: 7g | Proteins: 36g | Potassium: 560mg | Sodium: 350mg

Mexican Cauliflower Rice Bowl

🌿 *Prep time: 15 minutes*
🍲 *Cook time: 15 minutes*
🍽 *Servings: 4*

🍳 Ingredients:

- 1 large head of cauliflower, riced (about 4 cups)
- 1 tablespoon olive oil
- 1 small onion, finely chopped
- 2 cloves garlic, minced
- 1 red bell pepper, diced
- 1 jalapeño, seeds removed and finely chopped (optional, adjust to desired spiciness)
- 1 can (15 ounces) black beans, drained and rinsed
- 1 cup corn kernels (fresh, frozen, or canned)
- 1 teaspoon ground cumin
- 1 teaspoon chili powder
- 1/2 teaspoon smoked paprika
- Salt and pepper to taste
- 1 avocado, sliced
- Fresh cilantro, for garnish
- Lime wedges, for serving

🍴 Directions:

1. Remove the leaves and the abrasive core from the cauliflower head before beginning to rice it. Divide the florets, then put them in a food processor. Pulse the cauliflower until it resembles grains of rice. If you don't have a food processor, you may simply grate the cauliflower using a box grater.
2. The olive oil should be warmed in a large skillet over medium heat.
3. Place the finely diced onion in the skillet and simmer for 3–4 minutes, or until it becomes translucent.
4. Stir in the minced garlic, diced red bell pepper, and chopped jalapeño (if using). Cook everything together for another 2-3 minutes until the pepper starts to soften.
5. Add the riced cauliflower to the skillet. Cook it for about 5-6 minutes until it becomes tender, stirring occasionally.
6. Add the corn kernels and black beans. To fully reheat the beans and corn, cook everything together for an additional 2 to 3 minutes.

7. Add salt, pepper, cumin powder, smoked paprika, and chili powder to the Mexican Cauliflower Rice Bowl as seasonings. All the ingredients should be thoroughly mixed before serving.
8. Cook for another 1-2 minutes to allow the flavors to meld together.
9. Optional: Garnish the Mexican Cauliflower Rice Bowl with sliced avocado and fresh cilantro for added creaminess and herbal freshness.
10. Serve the flavorful and nutritious Mexican Cauliflower Rice Bowl with lime wedges on the side for a zesty touch!
11. Enjoy the wholesome and vibrant Mexican Cauliflower Rice Bowl as a satisfying and nourishing meal!

Nutritional Info Per Serving
(1/4 of the recipe, excluding optional items):

Calories: 280 | Fats: 10g | Carbs: 42g | Proteins: 11g | Potassium: 940mg | Sodium: 400mg

Herb-Marinated Grilled Pork Tenderloin

⅗ *Prep time: 15 minutes*

🍲 *Marinating time: 2 hours*

(or longer for more flavor)

🍽 *Cook time: 20 minutes*

🍴 *Servings: 4*

🍳 **Ingredients:**

- 2 pork tenderloins (about 1.5 pounds each)
- 1/4 cup olive oil
- 2 tablespoons balsamic vinegar
- 2 tablespoons fresh lemon juice
- 3 cloves garlic, minced
- 1 tablespoon chopped fresh rosemary
- 1 tablespoon chopped fresh thyme
- 1 tablespoon chopped fresh parsley
- 1 teaspoon dried oregano
- 1 teaspoon dried basil
- Salt and pepper to taste

🍳 **Directions:**

1. To make the herb marinade, combine the olive oil, balsamic vinegar, fresh lemon juice, minced garlic, chopped parsley, chopped thyme, dried oregano, and dried basil in a medium bowl. Season with salt and pepper.
2. Dry the pork tenderloins with paper towels.
3. Put the pork tenderloins in a large shallow dish or resealable plastic bag.
4. Pour the herb marinade over the pork tenderloins, making sure they are evenly coated.
5. For the best flavor infusion, marinate the pork in the fridge for at least two hours (or ideally overnight) by sealing the bag or covering the dish with plastic wrap.
6. Preheat your grill to medium-high heat.
7. Remove the marinated pork tenderloins from the refrigerator and let them sit at room temperature for about 15 minutes before grilling.
8. Grease the grill grates with a little olive oil to prevent sticking.
9. Cook the pork tenderloins on the prepared grill for 15 to 20 minutes, turning them over once or twice, or until an instant-read meat thermometer placed into the center of the meat reads 145°F (63°C).
10. Remove the grilled Herb-Marinated Pork Tenderloins from the grill and let them rest for about 5 minutes before slicing.
11. Slice the grilled pork tenderloins into thin medallions.
12. Serve the succulent and flavorful Herb-Marinated Grilled Pork Tenderloin with your choice of healthy sides, such as a green

salad or grilled vegetables, for a wholesome and delicious meal!

Nutritional Info Per Serving
(1/4 of the pork tenderloin, excluding optional items and serving side):
Calories: 340 | Fats: 19g | Carbs: 1g | Proteins: 38g | Potassium: 600mg | Sodium: 160mg

Mediterranean Zucchini Noodles with Shrimp

Prep time: 20 minutes

Cook time: 10 minutes

Servings: 4

Ingredients:

- 1 pound large shrimp, peeled and deveined
- 4 medium zucchinis
- 2 tablespoons olive oil
- 3 cloves garlic, minced
- 1 pint cherry tomatoes, halved
- 1/2 cup pitted Kalamata olives, sliced
- 1/4 cup crumbled feta cheese
- 2 tablespoons chopped fresh basil
- 2 tablespoons chopped fresh parsley
- 1 tablespoon lemon juice
- 1 teaspoon dried oregano
- Salt and pepper to taste

Directions:

1. Use a spiralizer or a vegetable peeler to make zucchini noodles from the medium zucchinis. Follow the manufacturer's instructions if using a spiralizer.
2. A large skillet is filled with 1 tablespoon of olive oil and heated to medium.
3. Stir in the minced garlic and heat it in the skillet for about a minute, or until it begins to smell delicious.
4. Add the peeled and deveined shrimp to the skillet. Cook them for two to three minutes on each side, or until they are fully cooked and pink. Don't overcook the shrimp. Take the cooked shrimp out of the skillet and set them aside.
5. Add the remaining 1 tablespoon of olive oil in the same skillet at medium heat.
6. Place the halved cherry tomatoes into the skillet. Sauté them for two to three minutes or until they begin to soften and release juices.
7. Stir in the sliced Kalamata olives and zucchini noodles. Cook everything together for another 2-3 minutes until the zucchini noodles are slightly softened.
8. Season the Mediterranean Zucchini Noodles with dried oregano, salt, and pepper. Mix all the ingredients together until the flavors are well combined.
9. Add the zucchini noodles and fried shrimp back to the skillet. Mix everything until well incorporated.
10. Drizzle the lemon juice over the skillet and toss it again to combine.
11. Stir in the crumbled feta cheese, chopped fresh basil, and chopped fresh parsley. Toss everything one last time until the feta cheese is slightly melted and the herbs are well distributed.
12. Optional: Garnish the Mediterranean Zucchini Noodles with Shrimp with additional fresh basil and parsley for added herbal fragrance.
13. Serve the delightful and protein-rich Mediterranean Zucchini Noodles with Shrimp as a wholesome and flavorful meal!

Nutritional Info Per Serving
(1/4 of the recipe, excluding optional items):
Calories: 290 | Fats: 14g | Carbs: 11g | Proteins: 30g | Potassium: 650mg | Sodium: 570mg

Thai Coconut Curry Chicken

Prep time: 20 minutes

Cook time: 25 minutes

Servings: 4

Ingredients:

- 1 pound boneless, skinless chicken breasts, cut into bite-sized pieces
- 1 tablespoon vegetable oil
- 1 tablespoon Thai red curry paste
- 1 can (13.5 ounces) coconut milk
- 1 cup chicken broth
- 2 tablespoons fish sauce (or soy sauce for a vegetarian option)
- 1 tablespoon brown sugar
- 1 red bell pepper, sliced
- 1 zucchini, sliced
- 1 cup sliced mushrooms
- 1 cup baby corn, halved
- 1 tablespoon fresh lime juice
- Fresh cilantro, for garnish
- Cooked rice, for serving

Directions:

1. In a big skillet or wok, heat the vegetable oil over medium-high heat.
2. Stir-fry the Thai red curry paste in the hot oil for approximately a minute, or until fragrant.
3. Add the bite-sized chicken pieces to the skillet, and cook them for about 4-5 minutes until they are browned on all sides and almost cooked through.
4. Add the brown sugar, coconut milk, chicken broth, fish sauce, and soy sauce. The curry sauce will boil gently after being thoroughly mixed.
5. Add the sliced red bell pepper, sliced zucchini, sliced mushrooms, and halved baby corn to the skillet and lower the heat to medium-low.
6. Boil the Thai Coconut Curry Chicken for 10 minutes or so, or until the chicken is fully cooked and the vegetables are tender.
7. Stir in the fresh lime juice to brighten up the flavors.
8. When necessary, add extra fish sauce (or soy sauce) and brown sugar after tasting the curry sauce to balance the spice.
9. Optional: Garnish the Thai Coconut Curry Chicken with fresh cilantro for added herbal fragrance.
10. Serve the aromatic and flavorful Thai Coconut Curry Chicken over cooked rice for a delicious and comforting meal!

Nutritional Info Per Serving
(1/4 of the recipe, excluding optional items and serving side):

Calories: 360 | Fats: 22g | Carbs: 15g | Proteins: 26g | Potassium: 720mg | Sodium: 800mg

Stuffed Bell Peppers with Turkey and Quinoa

Prep time: 20 minutes

Cook time: 50 minutes

Servings: 4

Ingredients:

- 4 large bell peppers (any color), tops removed, seeds and membranes removed
- 1 tablespoon olive oil
- 1 small onion, finely chopped
- 2 cloves garlic, minced
- 1 pound ground turkey
- 1 cup cooked quinoa
- 1 can (14.5 ounces) diced tomatoes, drained
- 1 teaspoon dried oregano
- 1 teaspoon dried basil
- 1/2 teaspoon ground cumin
- Salt and pepper to taste
- 1 cup shredded mozzarella cheese (or any preferred cheese)
- Fresh parsley, for garnish

⌧ Directions:

1. Set the oven temperature to 375°F (190°C).
2. In a large pot, bring water to a boil. The bell peppers should be blanched for 3 to 4 minutes, or until they are just beginning to soften, after being added whole. Keep the peppers after draining the water.
3. The olive oil should be warmed in a large skillet over medium heat.
4. Add the onion, which has been finely diced, to the skillet and cook it for 3–4 minutes, or until it turns translucent.
5. Add the minced garlic and stir; heat for an additional 30 seconds, or until fragrant.
6. With a spoon, crumble the ground turkey in the skillet. Roast the turkey until it is well-browned and done.
7. Mix in the cooked quinoa, drained diced tomatoes, dried oregano, dried basil, ground cumin, salt, and pepper. Let everything cook together for about 2-3 minutes to allow the flavors to meld.
8. Remove the skillet from the heat.
9. Stuff each blanched bell pepper with the turkey-quinoa mixture, pressing it down gently to fill them evenly.
10. In a baking dish, arrange the stuffed bell peppers standing up.
11. Optional: Sprinkle shredded mozzarella cheese over the top of each stuffed pepper.
12. Bake the stuffed bell peppers with turkey and quinoa in the preheated oven for about 25 to 30 minutes, or until the peppers are soft and the filling is well heated.
13. Take off the foil, and bake the filled peppers for an additional 5 to 10 minutes, or until the cheese (if used) is melted and bubbling.
14. Optional: Garnish the Stuffed Bell Peppers with fresh parsley for added herbal freshness.
15. Serve the wholesome and protein-packed Stuffed Bell Peppers with Turkey and Quinoa as a delightful and nutritious meal!

Nutritional Info Per Serving
(1 stuffed bell pepper, excluding optional items):

Calories: 370 | Fats: 14g | Carbs: 33g | Proteins: 29g | Potassium: 680mg | Sodium: 480mg

Pesto Zucchini Noodles with Grilled Chicken

🍴 *Prep time: 20 minutes*

🍲 *Cook time: 15 minutes*

🍽 *Servings: 4*

🥄 Ingredients:

- For the Pesto:
- 2 cups fresh basil leaves, packed
- 1/2 cup grated Parmesan cheese
- 1/3 cup pine nuts (or walnuts)
- 2 cloves garlic, minced
- 1/2 cup extra-virgin olive oil
- Salt and pepper to taste
- For the Zucchini Noodles:
- 4 medium zucchinis
- 2 tablespoons olive oil
- Salt and pepper to taste
- For the Grilled Chicken:
- 1 pound boneless, skinless chicken breasts
- 2 tablespoons olive oil
- 1 teaspoon dried oregano
- 1 teaspoon dried thyme
- 1 teaspoon garlic powder
- Salt and pepper to taste
- Optional toppings:
- Grated Parmesan cheese
- Fresh basil leaves

⌧ Directions:

1. For the Pesto:
2. Combine fresh basil leaves, grated Parmesan cheese, pine nuts (or

walnuts), garlic cloves, salt, and pepper in a food processor.

3. Pulse the ingredients until they are roughly chopped.
4. Pour the extra virgin olive oil in gradually while the food processor is running until the pesto is fully blended and smooth.
5. Taste the pesto and adjust the seasoning with more salt and pepper if needed.
6. Transfer the pesto to a bowl and set it aside.
7. For the Zucchini Noodles:
8. Create zucchini noodles from the medium zucchinis using a spiralizer or vegetable peeler. If using a spiralizer, follow the manufacturer's instructions.
9. The olive oil should be warmed in a large skillet over medium heat.
10. Add the zucchini noodles and mix well. Cook the noodles in the skillet for a few minutes, or until they soften. Add salt and pepper to the food according to taste.
11. Remove the skillet from the heat and set the zucchini noodles aside.
12. For the Grilled Chicken:
13. Set the temperature of your grill or grill pan to medium-high.
14. Place the boneless, skinless chicken breasts in a bowl and add the olive oil, salt, pepper, dried thyme, dried oregano, and dried oregano. The spice should be applied to the chicken in a uniform layer by tossing.
15. On the prepared grill, cook the chicken breasts for 5 to 6 minutes on each side, or until they are thoroughly cooked and have grill marks. A meat thermometer should read 165°F (74°C) when the internal temperature is checked.
16. Remove the grilled chicken from the grill and let it rest for a few minutes before slicing.
17. Assembly:
18. Combine the prepared pesto and the cooked zucchini noodles in a large mixing bowl. Mix everything together until the delightful pesto sauce is evenly distributed over the zucchini noodles.
19. Serve the Pesto Zucchini Noodles topped with sliced grilled chicken.
20. Optional: Garnish the dish with grated Parmesan cheese and fresh basil leaves for added flavor and presentation.
21. Enjoy the fresh and flavorful Pesto Zucchini Noodles with Grilled Chicken as a wholesome and satisfying meal!

Nutritional Info Per Serving
(1/4 of the recipe, excluding optional items):

Calories: 470 | Fats: 35g | Carbs: 9g | Proteins: 31g | Potassium: 900mg | Sodium: 320mg

Cucumber Dill Yogurt Bites

🥄 *Prep time: 15 minutes*

🍳 *Cook time: 0 minutes*

🍽 *Servings: 4*

Ingredients:

- 1 large cucumber
- 1 cup plain Greek yogurt
- 2 tablespoons fresh dill, chopped
- 1 tablespoon fresh lemon juice
- 1 clove garlic, minced
- Salt and pepper to taste
- Optional toppings: cherry tomatoes, olives, cucumber slices, fresh dill

Directions:

1. Wash and peel the cucumber. Cut it into thin rounds or slice it lengthwise to create cucumber boats.
2. Combine the plain Greek yogurt, fresh dill that has been chopped, fresh lemon juice, minced garlic, salt, and pepper in a bowl. To make the dill yogurt mixture, combine all ingredients.
3. Taste the dill yogurt mixture and adjust the seasoning with more salt and pepper if needed.
4. Using a spoon, place a dollop of the dill yogurt mixture onto each cucumber round or into each cucumber boat.
5. Optional: Top the Cucumber Dill Yogurt Bites with cherry tomatoes, olives, cucumber slices, or fresh dill for added texture and presentation.
6. Serve the refreshing and creamy Cucumber Dill Yogurt Bites as a delightful and light appetizer, snack, or side dish!

Nutritional Info Per Serving
(1/4 of the recipe, excluding optional toppings):

Calories: 60 | Fats: 2g | Carbs: 5g | Proteins: 6g | Potassium: 250mg | Sodium: 50mg

Lemon Herb Asparagus Spears

🥄 *Prep time: 10 minutes*

🍳 *Cook time: 15 minutes*

🍽 *Servings: 4*

Ingredients:

- 1 bunch fresh asparagus spears
- 1 tablespoon olive oil
- Zest of 1 lemon
- 2 tablespoons fresh lemon juice
- 2 cloves garlic, minced
- 1 tablespoon chopped fresh parsley
- 1 tablespoon chopped fresh thyme
- Salt and pepper to taste

Directions:

1. After washing, clip the tough ends off the asparagus spears by gently bending each spear until it breaks at the woody end while holding it at both ends.
2. To make the lemon herb marinade, combine the olive oil, lemon zest, lemon juice, minced garlic, fresh parsley, fresh thyme, salt, and pepper in a shallow dish.
3. Add the trimmed asparagus spears to the marinade, and toss them to coat evenly.
4. Let the asparagus marinate in the refrigerator for about 10 minutes to absorb the flavors.
5. The oven should be set to 425 °F (220 °C).

6. Line a baking sheet with parchment paper or lightly grease it with olive oil.
7. Arrange the marinated asparagus spears in a single layer on the prepared baking sheet.
8. Roast the Lemon Herb Asparagus Spears in the preheated oven for about 12-15 minutes until they are tender but still slightly crisp.
9. Optional: Garnish the roasted asparagus with additional chopped fresh parsley and lemon wedges for added freshness and presentation.
10. Serve the vibrant and zesty Lemon Herb Asparagus Spears as a delightful and nutritious appetizer, snack, or side dish!

Nutritional Info Per Serving
(1/4 of the recipe, excluding optional items):

Calories: 50 | Fats: 3g | Carbs: 5g | Proteins: 2g | Potassium: 230mg | Sodium: 2mg

Kale Chips with Sea Salt

✀ *Prep time: 10 minutes*

🍲 *Cook time: 15 minutes*

🍽 *Servings: 4*

🥄 **Ingredients:**

- 1 bunch of fresh kale
- 1 tablespoon olive oil
- Sea salt to taste

🔲 **Directions:**

1. Preheat your oven to 350°F (175°C).
2. Using a paper towel or a fresh kitchen towel, completely dry the kale leaves after giving them a good wash.
3. Cut the kale leaves into bite-sized pieces after removing the tough central stems.
4. In a large mixing bowl, combine the shredded kale leaves with the olive oil.

5. Toss the kale leaves in the olive oil until they are evenly coated.
6. Arrange the kale leaves on a parchment-lined baking sheet in a single layer.
7. Sprinkle sea salt over the kale leaves to taste.
8. Bake the Kale Chips in the preheated oven for about 12-15 minutes until they become crispy and lightly browned. Keep an eye on them as they can quickly go from crispy to burnt.
9. Before serving, let the kale chips cool for a few minutes after removing the baking sheet from the oven.
10. Serve the crispy and savory Kale Chips with Sea Salt as a delightful and guilt-free appetizer or snack!

Nutritional Info Per Serving
(1/4 of the recipe):

Calories: 60 | Fats: 4g | Carbs: 6g | Proteins: 2g | Potassium: 300mg | Sodium: 140mg

Mexican Cauliflower Rice

✀ *Prep time: 10 minutes*

🍲 *Cook time: 15 minutes*

🍽 *Servings: 4*

🥄 **Ingredients:**

- 1 large head of cauliflower
- 1 tablespoon olive oil
- 1 small onion, finely chopped
- 2 cloves garlic, minced
- 1 red bell pepper, diced
- 1 jalapeño, seeds removed and finely chopped (optional, adjust to spice preference)
- 1 can (14.5 ounces) diced tomatoes, drained
- 1 teaspoon ground cumin
- 1 teaspoon chili powder
- 1/2 teaspoon paprika
- Salt and pepper to taste
- Fresh cilantro, for garnish
- Lime wedges, for serving

⌧ Directions:

1. Wash the cauliflower head thoroughly and pat it dry. Remove the green leaves and the tough stem.
2. Cut the cauliflower into florets, and place them in a food processor.
3. In the food processor, pulse the cauliflower florets until they resemble rice-like grains. You want the texture to mimic rice, so take care not to overprocess.
4. In a large skillet, heat the olive oil over medium heat.
5. Add the finely chopped onion to the skillet, and sauté it for about 2-3 minutes until it becomes translucent.
6. Add the minced garlic and stir; heat for an additional 30 seconds, or until fragrant.
7. Fill the skillet with the diced red bell pepper and the chopped jalapenos. They should soften after 2 to 3 minutes of sautéing.
8. Add the riced cauliflower to the skillet, and stir everything together.
9. Mix in the drained diced tomatoes, ground cumin, chili powder, paprika, salt, and pepper.
10. When the cauliflower is tender but still slightly crunchy, cook the Mexican Cauliflower Rice for about 5-7 minutes, stirring every few minutes.
11. Taste the cauliflower rice and adjust the seasoning with more salt and pepper if needed.
12. Optional: Garnish the Mexican Cauliflower Rice with fresh cilantro for added herbal fragrance.
13. Serve the flavorful and low-carb Mexican Cauliflower Rice with lime wedges for a burst of citrusy freshness!

Nutritional Info Per Serving
(1/4 of the recipe, excluding optional items and serving side):

Calories: 80 | Fats: 3g | Carbs: 10g | Proteins: 4g | Potassium: 470mg | Sodium: 250mg

Baked Sweet Potato Fries

🍴 *Prep time: 15 minutes*

🍲 *Cook time: 25 minutes*

🍽 *Servings: 4*

🥄 Ingredients:

- 2 large sweet potatoes
- 2 tablespoons olive oil
- 1 teaspoon paprika
- 1/2 teaspoon garlic powder
- 1/2 teaspoon onion powder
- 1/2 teaspoon ground cumin
- 1/2 teaspoon salt
- Freshly ground black pepper to taste

⌧ Directions:

1. The oven should be set to 425 °F (220 °C). Grease a baking sheet with parchment paper or a little coating of olive oil.
2. Wash and peel the sweet potatoes. Cut them into evenly sized matchsticks or wedges.
3. The sweet potato matchsticks should be combined with olive oil, paprika, garlic powder, onion powder, ground cumin, salt, and black pepper in a big dish. Toss everything together until the seasoning is distributed evenly over the sweet potatoes.
4. Spread the seasoned sweet potato matchsticks in a single layer on the prepared baking sheet.
5. Bake the Baked Sweet Potato Fries in the preheated oven for about 20-25 minutes, flipping them halfway through, until they are crispy and lightly browned.
6. Before serving, let the sweet potato fries cool for a few minutes after

removing the baking sheet from the oven.

7. Serve the flavorful and wholesome Baked Sweet Potato Fries as a delightful and nutritious appetizer, snack, or side dish!

Nutritional Info Per Serving
(1/4 of the recipe, excluding optional items):

Calories: 150 | Fats: 7g | Carbs: 20g | Proteins: 2g | Potassium: 400mg | Sodium: 320mg

Roasted Garlic Brussels Sprouts

Prep time: 10 minutes

Cook time: 25 minutes

Servings: 4

Ingredients:

- 1 pound Brussels sprouts
- 3 tablespoons olive oil
- 4 cloves garlic, minced
- 1/2 teaspoon salt
- 1/4 teaspoon freshly ground black pepper
- 1/4 teaspoon red pepper flakes (optional, adjust to spice preference)

Directions:

1. Set the oven to 425 °F (220 °C). Grease a baking sheet with parchment paper or lightly coat it with olive oil.
2. Wash the Brussels sprouts thoroughly, and trim off the stem ends. Remove any loose or discolored outer leaves.
3. Cut the Brussels sprouts in half lengthwise, and place them in a large mixing bowl.
4. Combine olive oil, minced garlic, salt, pepper, and red pepper flakes (if used) in a small bowl.
5. After drizzling the Brussels sprouts with the garlic-infused oil mixture, toss them to fully coat them.

6. Spread the Brussels sprouts in a single layer on the prepared baking sheet.
7. Roast the Roasted Garlic Brussels Sprouts in the preheated oven for about 20-25 minutes, stirring halfway through, until they are tender and caramelized.
8. Before serving, let the roasted Brussels sprouts cool for a few minutes after removing the baking sheet from the oven.
9. Serve the aromatic and flavorful Roasted Garlic Brussels Sprouts as a delightful and nutritious appetizer, snack, or side dish!

Nutritional Info Per Serving
(1/4 of the recipe, excluding optional items):

Calories: 130 | Fats: 10g | Carbs: 10g | Proteins: 4g | Potassium: 470mg | Sodium: 300mg

Herb-Roasted Turnip Wedges

Prep time: 10 minutes

Cook time: 25 minutes

Servings: 4

Ingredients:

- 2 large turnips
- 2 tablespoons olive oil
- 1 teaspoon dried thyme
- 1 teaspoon dried rosemary
- 1/2 teaspoon garlic powder
- 1/2 teaspoon onion powder
- 1/2 teaspoon salt

Freshly ground black pepper to taste

Directions:

1. Turn on the oven to 425 °F (220 °C). Grease a baking sheet with a thin layer of olive oil or line it with parchment paper.
2. Wash and peel the turnips. Cut them into even-sized wedges or sticks.

3. In a large bowl, combine the turnip wedges with olive oil, dried thyme, dried rosemary, garlic powder, onion powder, salt, and black pepper. Toss everything together until the turnip wedges are evenly coated with the herb-infused olive oil mixture.
4. Spread the seasoned turnip wedges in a single layer on the prepared baking sheet.
5. When the Herb-Roasted Turnip Wedges are cooked and lightly browned, roast them in the preheated oven for 20 to 25 minutes, rotating them halfway through.
6. Take the baking sheet out of the oven and let the turnip wedges cool before serving.
7. Serve the flavorful and wholesome Herb-Roasted Turnip Wedges as a delightful and nutritious appetizer, snack, or side dish!

Nutritional Info Per Serving
(1/4 of the recipe, excluding optional items):

Calories: 70 | Fats: 5g | Carbs: 6g | Proteins: 1g | Potassium: 220mg | Sodium: 270mg

Mango Avocado Salsa

✂ Prep time: 15 minutes

🍲 Cook time: 0 minutes

🍽 Servings: 4

🥄 Ingredients:

- 1 large ripe mango, peeled, pitted, and diced
- 1 ripe avocado, peeled, pitted, and diced
- 1/2 small red onion, finely chopped
- 1 small jalapeño pepper, seeds removed and finely chopped
- 1/4 cup fresh cilantro, chopped
- 2 tablespoons fresh lime juice
- 1 tablespoon olive oil
- 1/2 teaspoon ground cumin
- Salt and pepper to taste

Directions:

1. In a medium mixing bowl, combine the diced mango, diced avocado, finely chopped red onion, finely chopped jalapeño, and chopped fresh cilantro.
2. The zesty dressing is made by combining the fresh lime juice, olive oil, ground cumin, salt, and pepper in a small bowl.
3. Pour the dressing over the mango and avocado mixture.
4. Gently toss all the ingredients together until the mango and avocado are evenly coated with the dressing.
5. Taste the Mango Avocado Salsa and adjust the seasoning with more salt and pepper if needed.
6. Let the salsa sit at room temperature for a few minutes to allow the flavors to meld.
7. Serve the vibrant and refreshing Mango Avocado Salsa as a delightful and nutritious appetizer, snack, or side dish!
8. Optional: You can add a squeeze of honey or a pinch of red pepper flakes if you prefer a touch of sweetness or extra spice.

Nutritional Info Per Serving
(1/4 of the recipe, excluding optional items):

Calories: 120 | Fats: 8g | Carbs: 14g | Proteins: 2g | Potassium: 320mg | Sodium: 10mg

Greek Yogurt Cucumber Dip

✂ Prep time: 10 minutes

🍲 Cook time: 0 minutes

🍽 Servings: 4

🥄 Ingredients:

- 1 cup plain Greek yogurt
- 1/2 cucumber, grated and

excess moisture squeezed out
- 2 cloves garlic, minced
- 1 tablespoon fresh lemon juice
- 1 tablespoon fresh dill, chopped
- 1 tablespoon fresh mint, chopped
- Salt and pepper to taste

📓 Directions:

1. In a medium mixing bowl, combine the plain Greek yogurt, grated cucumber, minced garlic, fresh lemon juice, chopped fresh dill, and chopped fresh mint.
2. Mix all the ingredients together until they are well incorporated.
3. Taste the Greek Yogurt Cucumber Dip and season with salt and pepper to your preference.
4. Optional: For a creamier consistency, you can refrigerate the dip for about 30 minutes before serving.
5. Serve the cool and refreshing Greek Yogurt Cucumber Dip as a delightful and healthy appetizer or snack!
6. Optional: You can also drizzle a little olive oil on top and garnish with additional fresh herbs for extra flavor and presentation.

Nutritional Info Per Serving
(1/4 of the recipe, excluding optional items):

Calories: 50 | Fats: 1g | Carbs: 4g | Proteins: 6g | Potassium: 140mg | Sodium: 30mg

Spicy Edamame

🥄 *Prep time: 5 minutes*
🥘 *Cook time: 5 minutes*
🍽 *Servings: 4*

🥄 Ingredients:

- 2 cups frozen edamame (immature soybeans), thawed
- 1 tablespoon sesame oil
- 1 tablespoon soy sauce
- 1 teaspoon chili flakes (adjust to spice preference)
- 1 teaspoon sesame seeds
- 1 green onion, thinly sliced (for garnish)

📓 Directions:

1. Before adding the thawed edamame, bring water in a medium-sized pot to a boil. To make the edamame soft, cook them for 3 to 4 minutes.
2. Drain the cooked edamame and transfer them to a large mixing bowl.
3. Mix the sesame oil, soy sauce, and chili flakes in a small bowl.
4. Pour the spicy sesame sauce over the edamame, and toss them gently to coat evenly.
5. Sprinkle sesame seeds over the Spicy Edamame and toss them again to incorporate the seeds.
6. Optional: Garnish the dish with thinly sliced green onions for added freshness and color.
7. Serve the zesty and protein-rich Spicy Edamame as a delightful and flavorful appetizer or snack!

Nutritional Info Per Serving
(1/4 of the recipe, excluding optional items):

Calories: 130 | Fats: 7g | Carbs: 9g | Proteins: 10g | Potassium: 240mg | Sodium: 320mg

Zucchini Noodle Salad with Lemon Dressing

🥄 *Prep time: 15 minutes*
🥘 *Cook time: 0 minutes*
🍽 *Servings: 4*

🥄 Ingredients:

- 4 medium zucchinis
- 1 cup cherry tomatoes, halved
- 1/2 red bell pepper, thinly sliced
- 1/4 red onion, thinly sliced
- 1/4 cup fresh basil leaves, torn

- 1/4 cup crumbled feta cheese (optional, omit for a dairy-free version)
- 2 tablespoons extra-virgin olive oil
- Juice of 1 lemon
- 1 clove garlic, minced
- 1/2 teaspoon Dijon mustard
- Salt and pepper to taste

Directions:

1. Thoroughly wash the zucchinis and trim the ends. Spiralize or peel the zucchinis into long, noodle-like strips with a vegetable peeler. Use a vegetable peeler to make broad, flat ribbons by running it down the length of the zucchini.
2. Combine the zucchini noodles, halved cherry tomatoes, red bell pepper, red onion, and torn fresh basil leaves in a large mixing bowl.
3. Combine the extra virgin olive oil, lemon juice, minced garlic, Dijon mustard, salt, and pepper in a small bowl to make the zesty lemon dressing.
4. Pour the lemon dressing over the zucchini noodle salad, and toss everything together until the salad is well coated.
5. Optional: Sprinkle crumbled feta cheese over the salad for added creaminess and tang. Skip this step for a dairy-free version.
6. Taste the Zucchini Noodle Salad and adjust the seasoning with more salt and pepper if needed.
7. Let the salad sit for a few minutes to allow the flavors to meld.
8. Serve the refreshing and vibrant Zucchini Noodle Salad with Lemon Dressing as a delightful and nutritious main or side dish!

Nutritional Info Per Serving
(1/4 of the recipe, excluding optional items):

Calories: 120 | Fats: 8g | Carbs: 10g | Proteins: 4g | Potassium: 460mg | Sodium: 90mg

Caprese Skewers with Balsamic Glaze

 Prep time: 15 minutes

 Cook time: 5 minutes

 Servings: 4

Ingredients:

- 1 pint cherry tomatoes
- 8 ounces fresh mozzarella cheese, cut into bite-sized pieces
- Fresh basil leaves
- Balsamic glaze (store-bought or homemade)
- Wooden skewers

Directions:

1. Wash the cherry tomatoes and pat them dry. Wash the fresh basil leaves and gently dry them with a paper towel.
2. Assemble the Caprese skewers by threading one cherry tomato, followed by a piece of fresh mozzarella, and a fresh basil leaf onto a wooden skewer. Repeat the process until all the ingredients are used.
3. Arrange the Caprese Skewers on a serving platter.
4. Drizzle balsamic glaze over the Caprese skewers. Use a pre-made balsamic glaze or create your own by thickening a balsamic vinegar reduction with a little honey or brown sugar.
5. Optional: Garnish the platter with additional fresh basil leaves for added aroma and presentation.
6. Serve the delightful and colorful Caprese Skewers with Balsamic Glaze as a refreshing and nutritious appetizer or party snack!

Nutritional Info Per Serving
(1/4 of the recipe, excluding optional items):

Calories: 160 | Fats: 10g | Carbs: 7g | Proteins: 12g | Potassium: 280mg | Sodium: 180mg

Eggplant and Tomato Stacks

Prep time: 15 minutes

Cook time: 20 minutes

Servings: 4

Ingredients:

- 1 large eggplant, sliced into 1/2-inch-thick rounds
- 2 large tomatoes, sliced into 1/2-inch-thick rounds
- 4 ounces fresh mozzarella cheese, sliced
- Fresh basil leaves
- 2 tablespoons balsamic glaze (store-bought or homemade)
- 2 tablespoons olive oil
- Salt and pepper to taste

Directions:

1. Set the oven temperature to 400°F (200°C). Grease a baking sheet with a thin layer of olive oil or line it with parchment paper.
2. Place the sliced eggplant on the baking sheet that has been prepared and brush both sides with olive oil. Add salt and pepper to taste.
3. Roast the eggplant slices in the preheated oven for about 15-20 minutes, flipping them halfway through, until they are tender and lightly browned.
4. Remove the eggplant rounds from the oven, and let them cool slightly.
5. Assemble the Eggplant and Tomato Stacks by layering one roasted eggplant round, followed by a tomato round, a slice of fresh mozzarella, and a fresh basil leaf. Repeat the process to create a stack, ending with a final eggplant round on top.
6. Drizzle the balsamic glaze over the Eggplant and Tomato Stacks.
7. Optional: Garnish the stacks with additional fresh basil leaves for added aroma and presentation.
8. Serve the delicious and colorful Eggplant and Tomato Stacks as a delightful and wholesome appetizer or side dish!

Nutritional Info Per Serving
(1/4 of the recipe, excluding optional items):

Calories: 190 | Fats: 13g | Carbs: 10g | Proteins: 8g | Potassium: 480mg | Sodium: 150mg

Smoked Salmon Cucumber Bites

Prep time: 15 minutes

Cook time: 0 minutes

Servings: 4

Ingredients:

- 1 large cucumber
- 4 ounces smoked salmon, thinly sliced
- 1/4 cup cream cheese (low-fat or regular)
- 1 tablespoon fresh dill, chopped
- 1 tablespoon fresh chives, chopped
- 1 teaspoon lemon juice
- Salt and pepper to taste

Directions:

1. Wash the cucumber thoroughly, and cut it into thick slices, about 1/2 inch in thickness.
2. Combine the cream cheese, lemon juice, chopped fresh chives, dill, and chives in a small bowl. Add a touch of salt and pepper to taste.
3. Top each slice of cucumber with a thin layer of the herbed cream cheese mixture.
4. Top each cucumber slice with a piece of thinly sliced smoked salmon.
5. Optional: Garnish the Smoked Salmon Cucumber Bites with additional fresh dill or chives for added flavor and presentation.

6. Serve the light and flavorful Smoked Salmon Cucumber Bites as a delightful and nutritious appetizer or party snack!

Quinoa Tabbouleh

🌾 *Prep time: 15 minutes*

🍲 *Cook time: 15 minutes*

🍽 *Servings: 4*

🥄 **Ingredients:**

- 1 cup quinoa
- 2 cups water
- 1 cup cucumber, diced
- 1 cup cherry tomatoes, halved
- 1/2 cup fresh parsley, chopped
- 1/4 cup fresh mint leaves, chopped
- 1/4 cup red onion, finely chopped
- 1/4 cup extra-virgin olive oil
- 2 tablespoons fresh lemon juice
- 1 clove garlic, minced
- Salt and pepper to taste

⌧ **Directions:**

1. Rinse the quinoa thoroughly under cold water.
2. Place two cups of water in a small pot and bring it to a roaring boil. After adding the rinsed quinoa, reduce the heat, cover the pan, and let the mixture simmer for about 15 minutes, or until the quinoa is cooked and the water has been absorbed. Before being allowed to cool, fluff the quinoa with a fork.
3. In a large mixing bowl, combine the cooked and cooled quinoa with diced cucumber, halved cherry tomatoes, chopped fresh parsley, chopped fresh mint leaves, and finely chopped red onion.
4. To make the tangy dressing, combine the extra-virgin olive oil, fresh lemon juice, minced garlic, salt, and pepper in a small bowl.
5. Pour the lemony dressing over the quinoa tabbouleh mixture, and toss everything together until the salad is well coated.
6. Taste the Quinoa Tabbouleh and adjust the seasoning with more salt and pepper if needed.
7. Let the salad sit for a few minutes to allow the flavors to meld.
8. Serve the refreshing and nutritious Quinoa Tabbouleh as a delightful and colorful main or side dish!

Baked Parmesan Zucchini Rounds

🌾 *Prep time: 10 minutes*

🍲 *Cook time: 20 minutes*

🍽 *Servings: 4*

🥄 **Ingredients:**

- 2 medium zucchini
- 1/4 cup grated Parmesan cheese
- 1/4 cup breadcrumbs (use whole wheat breadcrumbs for a healthier option)
- 1 teaspoon dried oregano
- 1/2 teaspoon garlic powder
- 1/4 teaspoon salt
- 1/4 teaspoon freshly ground black pepper
- 2 tablespoons olive oil
- Cooking spray (optional)

⌧ **Directions:**

1. Turn on the oven to 425 °F (220 °C). Lightly grease a baking sheet with cooking spray or line it with parchment paper.

2. Wash the zucchini thoroughly, and cut them into 1/4-inch-thick rounds.
3. In a shallow dish, combine the grated Parmesan cheese, breadcrumbs, dried oregano, garlic powder, salt, and black pepper.
4. Brush each zucchini round with olive oil on both sides.
5. Then press the zucchini rounds into the Parmesan mixture to evenly cover both sides.
6. Place the coated zucchini rounds on the prepared baking sheet in a single layer.
7. Optional: Lightly spray the tops of the zucchini rounds with cooking spray to help them get crispy during baking.
8. Bake the Baked Parmesan Zucchini Rounds in the preheated oven for about 18-20 minutes or until they are golden brown and crispy.
9. Before serving, let the zucchini rounds cool for a few minutes after removing the baking sheet from the oven.
10. Serve the flavorful and crunchy Baked Parmesan Zucchini Rounds as a delightful and healthy appetizer or side dish!

Nutritional Info Per Serving
(1/4 of the recipe, excluding optional items):

Calories: 140 | Fats: 9g | Carbs: 10g | Proteins: 5g | Potassium: 370mg | Sodium: 270mg

Desserts

Cinnamon Raisin Cookies

Prep time: 15 minutes

Cook time: 12 minutes

Servings: 12 cookies

Ingredients:

- 1 cup old-fashioned oats
- 1/2 cup whole wheat flour
- 1/4 cup raisins
- 1/4 cup chopped walnuts or almonds
- 1 teaspoon ground cinnamon
- 1/2 teaspoon baking powder
- 1/4 teaspoon salt
- 1/4 cup unsweetened applesauce
- 1/4 cup honey or maple syrup
- 1 large egg
- 1 teaspoon vanilla extract

Directions:

1. Turn the oven temperature up to 350 °F (175 °C). Either parchment paper or cooking spray can be used to lightly coat a baking sheet.
2. Mix the old-fashioned oats, whole wheat flour, raisins, chopped walnuts or almonds, ground cinnamon, baking soda, and salt in a large bowl.
3. Thoroughly mix the unsweetened applesauce, honey or maple syrup, egg, and vanilla extract in a different bowl.
4. Add the wet ingredients to the bowl of dry ingredients. Combine everything until the mixture resembles thick, sticky cookie dough.
5. Drop the cookie dough onto the preheated baking sheet with a tablespoon or ice cream scoop, leaving space between each cookie.
6. With the back of the spoon or your fingertips, slightly press down on each cookie.
7. Bake the cinnamon-raisin cookies for 10 to 12 minutes, or until the edges are just beginning to turn golden.
8. After a brief period of cooling on the baking sheet, the cookies should be transferred to a wire rack to complete cooling. The baking sheet needs to come out of the oven.
9. Serve the wholesome and naturally sweetened Cinnamon Raisin Cookies as a delightful and healthier dessert option!

Nutritional Info Per Serving (1 cookie):

Calories: 90 | Fats: 3g | Carbs: 14g | Proteins: 2g | Potassium: 85mg | Sodium: 50mg

Carrot Cake Bites

Prep time: 20 minutes

Chill time: 30 minutes

Servings: 12 bites

Ingredients:

- 1 cup grated carrots
- 1/2 cup old-fashioned oats
- 1/4 cup almond flour
- 1/4 cup chopped walnuts or pecans
- 1/4 cup shredded coconut (unsweetened)
- 1/4 cup raisins or dried cranberries
- 2 tablespoons honey or maple syrup
- 1 tablespoon coconut oil, melted
- 1 teaspoon ground cinnamon
- 1/2 teaspoon ground nutmeg
- 1/2 teaspoon vanilla extract
- Pinch of salt

Directions:

1. Combine the grated carrots, old-fashioned oats, almond flour,

chopped pecans or walnuts, shredded coconut, and raisins or dried cranberries in a large mixing bowl.
2. Combine the honey or maple syrup, melted coconut oil, ground cinnamon, ground nutmeg, vanilla extract, and a dash of salt in another bowl.
3. To create a sticky dough, combine the dry and wet ingredients.
4. To firm up the dough, place it in the refrigerator for about 30 minutes with the bowl covered with plastic wrap.
5. After chilling, use your hands to shape the dough into bite-sized balls.
6. Place the Carrot Cake Bites on a plate or tray lined with parchment paper.
7. Optional: For added sweetness and presentation, you can roll the bites in a little extra shredded coconut.
8. Refrigerate the Carrot Cake Bites for another 15-20 minutes before serving to set.
9. Serve the naturally sweet and nutty Carrot Cake Bites as a delightful and guilt-free dessert or snack!

Nutritional Info Per Serving (1 bite):

Calories: 90 | Fats: 5g | Carbs: 10g | Proteins: 2g | Potassium: 100mg | Sodium: 10mg

Almond Butter Brownies

🥄 *Prep time: 15 minutes*

🍳 *Cook time: 25 minutes*

🍴 *Servings: 16 brownies*

Ingredients:

- 1 cup creamy almond butter (unsweetened)
- 1/2 cup honey or maple syrup
- 2 large eggs
- 1 teaspoon vanilla extract
- 1/2 cup unsweetened cocoa powder
- 1/4 teaspoon baking soda
- Pinch of salt
- 1/3 cup dark chocolate chips (optional, for added richness)

Directions:

1. Set the oven temperature to 350°F (175°C). Use cooking spray to grease an 8x8-inch baking sheet or line it with parchment paper.
2. Combine the eggs, vanilla extract, honey or maple syrup, and smooth almond butter in a big mixing bowl. The ingredients should be thoroughly mixed and smooth after being whisked.
3. Add a dash of salt, baking soda, and unsweetened cocoa powder to the wet ingredients. Once you have a thick and fudgy brownie batter, stir everything together.
4. Optional: Fold in the dark chocolate chips for an extra burst of chocolatey goodness.
5. Spread the brownie batter evenly across the prepared baking pan.
6. A toothpick inserted in the center of the prepared Almond Butter Brownies should come out with a few moist crumbs after 20 to 25 minutes of baking.
7. Take the baking pan out of the oven, and leave the brownies to cool entirely inside.
8. Once cooled, slice the brownies into 16 squares.
9. Serve the rich and decadent Almond Butter Brownies as a delightful and slightly healthier dessert option!

Nutritional Info Per Serving (1 brownie):

Calories: 170 | Fats: 10g | Carbs: 17g | Proteins: 5g | Potassium: 130mg | Sodium: 55mg

Lemon Chia Seed Pudding

🌿 *Prep time: 10 minutes*

🍲 *Chill time: 4 hours or overnight*

🍮 *Servings: 4*

🍵 Ingredients:

- 1/2 cup chia seeds
- 2 cups unsweetened almond milk (or any milk of your choice)
- Zest of 1 lemon
- Juice of 1 lemon
- 2 tablespoons honey or maple syrup (adjust to taste)
- 1/2 teaspoon vanilla extract
- Fresh berries and lemon slices for garnish (optional)

❎ Directions:

1. Combine chia seeds, unsweetened almond milk, lemon zest, lemon juice, honey, maple syrup, and vanilla extract in a mixing bowl. Stir everything thoroughly until well combined.
2. Let the mixture sit for a few minutes, then stir again to prevent clumping.
3. The Lemon Chia Seed Pudding must be chilled for at least 4 hours or overnight so that the chia seeds can absorb the liquid and thicken. To stop evaporation, cover the bowl with plastic wrap or a different cover.
4. After the chilling time, give the pudding a good stir to ensure a smooth and consistent texture.
5. Divide the Lemon Chia Seed Pudding into serving bowls or glasses.
6. Optional: Garnish with fresh berries and lemon slices for added color and freshness.
7. Serve the tangy and creamy Lemon Chia Seed Pudding as a delightful and nutritious dessert or breakfast option!

Nutritional Info Per Serving
(1/4 of the recipe, excluding optional items):

Calories: 170 | Fats: 8g | Carbs: 20g | Proteins: 6g | Potassium: 210mg | Sodium: 80mg

Walnut Oatmeal Bars

🌿 *Prep time: 15 minutes*

🍲 *Cook time: 25 minutes*

🍮 *Servings: 12 bars*

🍵 Ingredients:

- 1 1/2 cups old-fashioned oats
- 3/4 cup whole wheat flour
- 1/2 cup chopped walnuts
- 1/4 cup honey or maple syrup
- 1/4 cup unsweetened applesauce
- 2 tablespoons coconut oil, melted
- 1 teaspoon ground cinnamon
- 1/2 teaspoon baking soda
- Pinch of salt
- 1/2 cup unsweetened applesauce
- 1 teaspoon vanilla extract

❎ Directions:

1. Set the oven temperature to 350°F (175°C). Use cooking spray or parchment paper to grease or line an 8x8-inch baking sheet.
2. Combine the old-fashioned oats, whole wheat flour, chopped walnuts, ground cinnamon, baking soda, and a dash of salt in a large mixing bowl.
3. Mix the honey or maple syrup, unsweetened applesauce, melted coconut oil, and vanilla extract thoroughly in a another bowl.
4. Combine all the ingredients until you have a sticky dough by pouring the wet ingredients over the dry ones.
5. Press about two-thirds of the dough into the bottom of the prepared baking pan to form the bottom layer of the bars.

6. Spread the unsweetened applesauce evenly over the bottom layer of the dough.
7. Crumble the remaining dough over the applesauce to create the top layer of the bars.
8. Bake the Walnut Oatmeal Bars in the preheated oven for about 20-25 minutes or until they are golden brown around the edges.
9. Take the baking pan out of the oven, and leave the bars to cool entirely inside.
10. After the bars have cooled, cut them into 12 squares.
11. Serve the wholesome and naturally sweetened Walnut Oatmeal Bars as a delightful and slightly healthier dessert or snack!

Nutritional Info Per Serving
(1 bar):

Calories: 170 | Fats: 8g | Carbs: 21g | Proteins: 3g | Potassium: 90mg | Sodium: 40mg

Raspberry Swirl Cheesecake Bars

Prep time: 20 minutes

Cook time: 40 minutes

Chill time: 4 hours or overnight

Servings: 12 bars

Ingredients:

- *For the crust:*
- 1 cup graham cracker crumbs
- 2 tablespoons unsalted butter, melted
- 1 tablespoon honey or maple syrup
- For the cheesecake filling:
- 16 ounces cream cheese, softened (use low-fat cream cheese for a healthier option)
- 1/2 cup Greek yogurt (plain, unsweetened)
- 1/2 cup granulated sugar or sweetener of choice
- 2 large eggs
- 1 teaspoon vanilla extract
- For the raspberry swirl:
- 1 cup fresh or frozen raspberries
- 2 tablespoons granulated sugar or sweetener of choice
- 1 tablespoon water

Directions:

1. Set the oven temperature to 325°F (160°C). Lightly grease an 8x8-inch baking sheet with cooking spray or line it with parchment paper.
2. In a mixing bowl, combine the broken graham crackers, melted unsalted butter, and honey or maple syrup. The crumbs should be thoroughly mixed and coated.
3. Make a uniform layer by pressing the crust mixture firmly into the prepared baking pan.
4. The softened cream cheese, Greek yogurt, granulated sugar, eggs, and vanilla extract should all be combined in a different, large mixing bowl and combined until smooth and creamy.
5. Pour the cheesecake filling over the crust in the baking pan.
6. Combine the raspberries, water, and granulated sugar in a small saucepan. Mash the raspberries with a spoon as you cook the mixture over medium heat until it thickens into a sauce.
7. Drizzle raspberry sauce in dollops over the cheesecake filling.
8. To achieve a marbled appearance, carefully fold the raspberry sauce into the cheesecake filling using a butter knife.
9. Bake the Raspberry Swirl Cheesecake Bars in the preheated oven for about 35-40 minutes or until the edges are set and the center is slightly jiggly.
10. After removing the baking pan from the oven, let the bars to finish cooling in it.
11. After they have cooled, wrap the pan in plastic wrap and place it in

the refrigerator for at least 4 hours or overnight to chill and set the bars.

12. After they've chilled, use the parchment paper as handles to pull the bars out of the pan and cut them into 12 squares.

13. Serve the luscious and fruity Raspberry Swirl Cheesecake Bars as a delightful and indulgent dessert!

Nutritional Info Per Serving
(1 bar):

Calories: 230 | Fats: 16g | Carbs: 18g | Proteins: 5g | Potassium: 120mg | Sodium: 200mg

Quinoa Chocolate Chip Cookies

Prep time: 20 minutes

Cook time: 12 minutes

Servings: 24 cookies

Ingredients:

- 1 cup cooked quinoa, cooled
- 1 cup whole wheat flour
- 1/2 cup unsalted butter, softened
- 1/2 cup honey or maple syrup
- 1 large egg
- 1 teaspoon vanilla extract
- 1/2 teaspoon baking soda
- 1/4 teaspoon salt
- 3/4 cup dark chocolate chips

Directions:

1. Set the oven temperature to 350°F (175°C). Lightly grease a baking sheet with cooking spray or line it with parchment paper.

2. In a large mixing bowl, thoroughly mix the honey or maple syrup and softened unsalted butter.

3. Stir the mixture until it is smooth after adding the egg and vanilla extract.

4. In another bowl, mix the salt, baking soda, and whole wheat flour.

5. Gradually add the dry ingredients to the wet ingredients until just incorporated.

6. Gently fold in the dark chocolate chips and cooked quinoa that has cooled into the cookie dough.

7. Leave room between each cookie as you drop rounded spoonful's of cookie dough onto the prepared baking sheet.

8. Press down each cookie slightly with the back of the spoon.

9. Place the quinoa chocolate chip cookies in the preheated oven and bake them for 10 to 12 minutes, or until the edges are just beginning to turn golden.

10. After a brief period of cooling on the baking sheet, the cookies should be transferred to a wire rack to complete cooling. The baking sheet needs to come out of the oven.

11. Serve the chewy and nutritious Quinoa Chocolate Chip Cookies as a delightful and slightly healthier dessert or snack!

Nutritional Info Per Serving
(1 cookie):

Calories: 120 | Fats: 6g | Carbs: 14g | Proteins: 2g | Potassium: 70mg | Sodium: 60mg

Pear and Almond Crumble

Prep time: 20 minutes

Cook time: 35 minutes

Servings: 6

Ingredients:

- For the filling:
- 4 ripe pears, peeled, cored, and sliced
- 2 tablespoons honey or maple syrup
- 1 tablespoon lemon juice
- 1 teaspoon ground cinnamon
- 1/4 teaspoon ground nutmeg

- For the crumble topping:
- 1/2 cup rolled oats
- 1/4 cup almond flour
- 1/4 cup chopped almonds
- 2 tablespoons unsalted butter, softened
- 2 tablespoons honey or maple syrup
- 1/2 teaspoon ground cinnamon
- Pinch of salt

⌧ Directions:

1. Set your oven temperature to 375°F (190°C). Grease an 8x8-inch baking dish with butter or cooking spray.
2. In a large mixing bowl, gently toss the sliced pears with honey or maple syrup, lemon juice, ground cinnamon, and ground nutmeg until the pears are well coated.
3. Transfer the pear mixture to the prepared baking dish, spreading it out evenly.
4. Rolling oats, almond flour, chopped almonds, softened unsalted butter, honey or maple syrup, ground cinnamon, and a dash of salt should all be combined in a separate bowl. Mix everything until the crumble topping is fully mixed and crumbly.
5. Sprinkle the crumble topping over the pear filling in the baking dish, covering the pears evenly.
6. Bake the Pear and Almond Crumble in the preheated oven for about 30-35 minutes or until the top is golden brown and the pears are tender.
7. Take the baking dish out of the oven, then wait for the crumble to cool slightly before serving.
8. As a delicious and healthy dessert option, serve the warm and soothing Pear and Almond Crumble!

Nutritional Info Per Serving
(1/6 of the recipe):

Calories: 260 | Fats: 11g | Carbs: 39g | Proteins: 4g | Potassium: 250mg | Sodium: 20mg

Sweet Potato Pie Bites

🍲 *Prep time: 30 minutes*

🍳 *Cook time: 25 minutes*

🍽 *Servings: 24 bites*

⌧ Ingredients:

- For the crust:
- 1 cup whole wheat flour
- 1/2 cup unsalted butter, cold and cubed
- 2 tablespoons honey or maple syrup
- 1/4 teaspoon salt
- 1-2 tablespoons ice water
- For the sweet potato filling:
- 1 cup cooked and mashed sweet potato (about 1 medium-sized sweet potato)
- 1/4 cup honey or maple syrup
- 1/2 cup unsweetened almond milk (or any milk of your choice)
- 1 large egg
- 1 teaspoon ground cinnamon
- 1/2 teaspoon ground nutmeg
- 1/4 teaspoon ground ginger
- 1/4 teaspoon salt
- 1 teaspoon vanilla extract

⌧ Directions:

1. For the crust:
2. Place the whole wheat flour, cold, cubed, unsalted butter, honey or maple syrup, and salt in a food processor. Pulse the ingredients only until it resembles coarse crumbs.
3. Continue pulsing after each addition of 1 tablespoon ice water until the dough comes together. For the proper consistency, 1 to 2 teaspoons of ice water may be required.

4. Shape the dough into a ball, slightly press it down, cover it with plastic wrap, and chill it for 15 minutes.
5. For the sweet potato filling:
6. Set the oven temperature to 350°F (175°C). Spray cooking oil in a tiny muffin tray.
7. Combine the cooked and mashed sweet potato with the honey, maple syrup, unsweetened almond milk, egg, cinnamon, nutmeg, ginger, salt, and vanilla extract in a mixing bowl. Stir the filling until it's well combined and smooth.
8. Assembling the Sweet Potato Pie Bites:
9. On a lightly floured surface, roll out the chilled dough to about 1/8-inch thickness.
10. To make circles of dough that fit into the wells of the small muffin tin, use a round cookie cutter or a glass.
11. To create miniature pie crusts, press each round of dough into the wells.
12. Spoon a small amount of the sweet potato filling into each pie crust.
13. Bake the Sweet Potato Pie Bites in the preheated oven for about 20-25 minutes or until the crusts are golden and the filling is set.
14. Before transferring the pie pieces to a wire rack to complete cooling, allow them to cool in the little muffin pan for a few minutes.
15. Serve the adorable and flavorful Sweet Potato Pie Bites as a delightful and healthier dessert option!

Nutritional Info Per Serving
(1 bite):

Calories: 90 | Fats: 4g | Carbs: 12g | Proteins: 2g | Potassium: 70mg | Sodium: 45mg

Orange Date Energy Balls

🍽 *Prep time: 15 minutes*

🍴 *Chill time: 30 minutes*

🍽 *Servings: 12 energy balls*

Ingredients:

- 1 cup dates, pitted and soaked in warm water for 10 minutes
- 1 cup old-fashioned oats
- 1/2 cup unsweetened shredded coconut
- 1/4 cup raw almonds
- Zest of 1 orange
- 2 tablespoons orange juice
- 1 tablespoon chia seeds
- 1/2 teaspoon vanilla extract
- Pinch of salt
- Optional coating:
- 2 tablespoons unsweetened shredded coconut

Directions:

1. Combine the soaked dates, old-fashioned oats, unsweetened coconut shreds, raw almonds, orange zest, orange juice, chia seeds, vanilla extract, and a dash of salt in a food processor.
2. Pulse the ingredients until they form a sticky and well-combined mixture. The mixture should hold together when pinched.
3. Take small portions of the mixture and roll them into balls between your palms. If desired, roll the energy balls in unsweetened shredded coconut for an extra coating.
4. Place the Orange Date Energy Balls on a plate or tray lined with parchment paper.
5. Optional: Refrigerate the energy balls for about 30 minutes to firm them up.
6. Serve the naturally sweet and zesty Orange Date Energy Balls as a delightful and energizing snack or dessert!

Spiced Fig Compote

Prep time: 10 minutes

Cook time: 20 minutes

*Servings: Approximately 12
servings*

Ingredients:

- 1 pound fresh figs,
  stemmed and quartered
- 1/4 cup honey or maple syrup
- 1/4 cup water
- 1 cinnamon stick
- 2 whole cloves
- 1/4 teaspoon ground ginger
- 1/4 teaspoon ground nutmeg
- 1/4 teaspoon vanilla extract
- Zest of 1 orange (optional,
  for added flavor)

Directions:

1. In a saucepan, combine the
   quartered fresh figs, honey or
   maple syrup, water, cinnamon
   stick, whole cloves, ground ginger,
   and ground nutmeg.
2. Optional: Add the orange zest for
   an extra burst of flavor.
3. Over medium heat, simmer the
   mixture while occasionally stirring.
4. Reduce the heat to low and let the
   Spiced Fig Compote gently simmer
   for about 15-20 minutes or until
   the figs are soft and the mixture
   has thickened to a compote-like
   consistency.
5. Remove the whole cloves and
   cinnamon stick from the compote.
6. Stir in the vanilla extract.
7. Let the Spiced Fig Compote cool
   slightly before transferring it to a
   jar or container.

8. Serve the fragrant and spiced
   Spiced Fig Compote as a delightful
   and versatile topping for yogurt,
   oatmeal, pancakes, waffles, or as
   a delicious accompaniment to
   cheese!
9. Store any leftover compote in the
   refrigerator for up to one week.

Coconut Flour Pancakes with Berries

Prep time: 10 minutes

Cook time: 10 minutes

*Servings: Approximately 6
pancakes*

Ingredients:

- 1/2 cup coconut flour
- 1/2 teaspoon baking powder
- Pinch of salt
- 4 large eggs
- 1/2 cup unsweetened
  almond milk (or any
  milk of your choice)
- 2 tablespoons honey
  or maple syrup
- 1 teaspoon vanilla extract
- Cooking spray or coconut
  oil, for greasing the pan
- Fresh berries (such as
  blueberries, strawberries, or
  raspberries), for serving
- Maple syrup or honey, for
  drizzling (optional)

Directions:

1. Combine the coconut flour, baking
   soda, and a dash of salt in a mixing
   dish.
2. Combine the eggs, unsweetened
   almond milk, honey or maple
   syrup, and vanilla extract in
   another bowl.

3. Gradually combine the wet and dry ingredients while mixing the mixture to create a homogeneous batter. You can thin out the batter if it is too thick by adding a little more almond milk.
4. Set a nonstick griddle or skillet to medium heat. Grease the surface just a bit with coconut oil or cooking spray.
5. To make a pancake, pour 1/4 cup of the pancake batter into the skillet. Cook for two to three minutes on each side, or until surface bubbles appear and the edges are set.
6. Flip the pancake and cook the other side until it is golden brown.
7. Repeat the process with the remaining batter to make approximately 6 pancakes.
8. Serve the Coconut Flour Pancakes with a handful of fresh berries on top.
9. Optional: Drizzle with a little maple syrup or honey for added sweetness.
10. Enjoy these fluffy and nutritious Coconut Flour Pancakes with Berries as a delightful and guilt-free breakfast treat!

Nutritional Info Per Serving
(1 pancake, excluding toppings):

Calories: 110 | Fats: 5g | Carbs: 11g | Proteins: 5g | Potassium: 90mg | Sodium: 80mg

Vanilla Raspberry Parfait

🍴 *Prep time: 15 minutes*

🍲 *Chill time: 1 hour*

🍽 *Servings: 2 parfaits*

🥣 **Ingredients:**

- 1 cup plain Greek yogurt (unsweetened)
- 1 tablespoon honey or maple syrup
- 1 teaspoon vanilla extract
- 1 cup fresh raspberries
- 1/4 cup granola (choose a low-sugar or unsweetened variety)
- Optional toppings:
- Fresh mint leaves
- Additional raspberries

🍴 **Directions:**

1. Mix the plain Greek yogurt plain, honey (or maple syrup), and vanilla extract in a small bowl.
2. Take two parfait glasses or tall glasses and start layering the Vanilla Raspberry Parfait. Begin with a spoonful of the sweetened yogurt at the bottom of each glass.
3. Add a layer of fresh raspberries on top of the yogurt.
4. Sprinkle a layer of granola over the raspberries.
5. Repeat the layering process with another spoonful of yogurt, more raspberries, and another layer of granola until you reach the top of the glasses.
6. Add a few additional fresh raspberries and, if preferred, a sprig of fresh mint to the parfaits to give them a last touch of color and freshness.
7. Cover the parfait glasses and refrigerate the Vanilla Raspberry Parfait for at least 1 hour to chill and allow the flavors to meld.
8. Once chilled, serve the creamy and fruity Vanilla Raspberry Parfait as a delightful and refreshing dessert or breakfast treat!

Nutritional Info Per Serving
(1 parfait):

Calories: 250 | Fats: 4g | Carbs: 40g | Proteins: 16g | Potassium: 270mg | Sodium: 65mg

Chai Spiced Rice Pudding

🍴 *Prep time: 10 minutes*

🍲 *Cook time: 30 minutes*

🍲 *Chill time: 2 hours (optional)*

🍽 *Servings: 4*

⚗ Ingredients:

- 1/2 cup white rice (short-grain or long-grain)
- 2 cups milk (dairy or non-dairy such as almond milk or coconut milk)
- 2 tablespoons honey or maple syrup
- 1 cinnamon stick
- 2-3 whole cloves
- 2-3 cardamom pods, lightly crushed
- 1/4 teaspoon ground cinnamon
- 1/4 teaspoon ground ginger
- 1/8 teaspoon ground nutmeg
- Pinch of salt
- 1/2 teaspoon vanilla extract
- 1/4 cup raisins (optional, for added sweetness and texture)
- Chopped pistachios or almonds for garnish

✂ Directions:

1. In a saucepan, rinse the white rice under cold water until the water runs clear. Drain the rice and set it aside.
2. Place the milk, honey or maple syrup, cinnamon stick, whole cloves, cardamom pods that have been crushed, ground cinnamon, ground ginger, ground nutmeg, and a dash of salt in the same saucepan.
3. Over medium-low heat, gently simmer the milk mixture, stirring now and again to avoid burning or sticking.
4. Stir the washed white rice into the milk mixture before adding it. For about 25 to 30 minutes, or until the rice is mushy and the mixture has thickened to a creamy consistency, cook the rice pudding over low heat while stirring periodically.
5. Optional: Stir in the vanilla extract and raisins for added sweetness and texture.
6. Remove the cinnamon stick, whole cloves, and ground cardamom pods from the pan when the heat has been turned off.
7. You can let the Chai Spiced Rice Pudding cool a little before serving. Alternatively, you can chill the rice pudding for at least two hours if you want a cold version.
8. Serve the fragrant and spiced Chai Spiced Rice Pudding in individual bowls or glasses, garnished with chopped pistachios or almonds for a delightful and comforting dessert!

Nutritional Info Per Serving
(1/4 of the recipe):

Calories: 230 | Fats: 5g | Carbs: 42g | Proteins: 6g | Potassium: 240mg | Sodium: 95mg

Smoothies

Spinach and Pineapple Smoothie

⏱ *Prep time: 5 minutes*

🍲 *Cook time: 0 minutes*

🍽 *Servings: 2*

🥣 **Ingredients:**

- 2 cups fresh spinach leaves
- 1 cup fresh or frozen pineapple chunks
- 1 ripe banana
- 1 cup unsweetened almond milk (or any milk of your choice)
- 1 tablespoon chia seeds
- 1 teaspoon honey or maple syrup (optional, for added sweetness)
- Ice cubes (optional, if using fresh pineapple and you prefer a colder smoothie)

🗒 **Directions:**

1. Add the fresh spinach leaves, pineapple chunks, ripe banana, chia seeds, and unsweetened almond milk to a blender.
2. If you'd like, you can add sweetness by adding honey or maple syrup. Keep in mind that the natural sweetness of the fruits may be adequate.
3. Combine all the ingredients in a blender and process until they are smooth and creamy. If you want a colder smoothie and you're using fresh pineapple, you can add a couple of ice cubes and blend again.
4. Taste the smoothie and adjust sweetness or consistency as per your preference.
5. Pour the Spinach and Pineapple Smoothie into two glasses.
6. Serve the refreshing and nutrient-rich Spinach and Pineapple Smoothie as a delightful and healthy breakfast or snack!

Nutritional Info Per Serving:
Calories: 130 | Fats: 3g | Carbs: 26g | Proteins: 3g | Potassium: 430mg | Sodium: 100mg

Mango-Coconut Smoothie

⏱ *Prep time: 5 minutes*

🍲 *Cook time: 0 minutes*

🍽 *Servings: 2*

🥣 **Ingredients:**

- 2 cups ripe mango chunks (fresh or frozen)
- 1 cup unsweetened coconut milk (canned or carton)
- 1/2 cup plain Greek yogurt (unsweetened)
- 1 tablespoon honey or maple syrup (optional, for added sweetness)
- 1/2 teaspoon vanilla extract
- Ice cubes (optional, if using fresh mango and you prefer a colder smoothie)
- Toasted coconut flakes (for garnish, optional)

🗒 **Directions:**

1. Add the ripe mango chunks, unsweetened coconut milk, plain Greek yogurt, and vanilla extract to a blender.
2. If you'd like, you can increase the sweetness by adding honey or maple syrup. The natural sweetness of the mature mango may be sufficient.
3. Combine all ingredients in a blender and process until they are smooth and creamy.
4. If you're using fresh mango and want a colder smoothie, add a few ice cubes and re-blend the mixture.
5. Taste the smoothie and adjust sweetness or consistency as per your preference.

6. Pour the Mango-Coconut Smoothie into two glasses.
7. Optional: For an extra touch of tropical flavor, garnish with toasted coconut flakes.
8. Serve the tropical and refreshing Mango-Coconut Smoothie as a delightful and healthy breakfast or snack!

Nutritional Info Per Serving:
Calories: 180 | Fats: 6g | Carbs: 30g | Proteins: 6g | Potassium: 370mg | Sodium: 35mg

Cucumber Melon Smoothie

🕙 *Prep time: 5 minutes*

🍲 *Cook time: 0 minutes*

🍽 *Servings: 2*

Ingredients:

- 1 cup diced cucumber (peeled and seeds removed)
- 1 cup diced honeydew melon
- 1 cup diced cantaloupe melon
- 1/2 cup plain Greek yogurt (unsweetened)
- 1 tablespoon honey or maple syrup (optional, for added sweetness)
- 1/2 lime, juiced
- Fresh mint leaves (for garnish, optional)
- Ice cubes (optional, for a colder smoothie)

Directions:

1. Add the diced cucumber, honeydew melon, cantaloupe melon, plain Greek yogurt, and lime juice to a blender.
2. If you'd like, you can increase the sweetness by adding honey or maple syrup. The natural sweetness of the melons may be sufficient.
3. Combine all the ingredients in a blender and process until they are smooth and creamy.

4. You can blend the smoothie again after adding some ice cubes if you want it to be colder.
5. Taste the smoothie and adjust sweetness or consistency as per your preference.
6. Pour the Cucumber Melon Smoothie into two glasses.
7. Optional: Garnish with fresh mint leaves for a refreshing touch.
8. Serve the hydrating and delightful Cucumber Melon Smoothie as a healthy and cooling breakfast or snack!

Nutritional Info Per Serving:
Calories: 100 | Fats: 1g | Carbs: 20g | Proteins: 5g | Potassium: 400mg | Sodium: 35mg

Berry Chia Smoothie

🕙 *Prep time: 5 minutes*

🍲 *Cook time: 0 minutes*

🍽 *Servings: 2*

Ingredients:

- 1 cup mixed berries (such as strawberries, blueberries, and raspberries) (fresh or frozen)
- 1 cup unsweetened almond milk (or any milk of your choice)
- 2 tablespoons chia seeds
- 1 tablespoon honey or maple syrup (optional, for added sweetness)
- 1/2 teaspoon vanilla extract
- Ice cubes (optional, if using fresh berries and you prefer a colder smoothie)

Directions:

1. Add the mixed berries, unsweetened almond milk, chia seeds, and vanilla extract to a blender.
2. If you'd like, you can increase the sweetness by adding honey or maple syrup. The sweetness

of the berries themselves may be sufficient.

3. Combine all the ingredients in a blender and process until you have a smooth, vivid purple smoothie.
4. You can blend the smoothie again after adding some ice cubes if you want it to be colder.
5. Taste the smoothie and adjust sweetness or consistency as per your preference.
6. Pour the Berry Chia Smoothie into two glasses.
7. Serve the antioxidant-rich and nutritious Berry Chia Smoothie as a delicious and energizing breakfast or snack!

Nutritional Info Per Serving:

Calories: 120 | Fats: 4g | Carbs: 18g | Proteins: 3g | Potassium: 220mg | Sodium: 80mg

Kiwi Lime Smoothie

🕰 *Prep time: 5 minutes*

🍲 *Cook time: 0 minutes*

🍽 *Servings: 2*

🥤 **Ingredients:**

- 2 ripe kiwis, peeled and sliced
- Juice of 1 lime
- 1 cup baby spinach leaves
- 1 cup unsweetened coconut water (or any liquid of your choice)
- 1 tablespoon chia seeds
- 1 tablespoon honey or maple syrup (optional, for added sweetness)
- Ice cubes (optional, for a colder smoothie)
- Slices of kiwi and lime for garnish (optional)

🍴 Directions:

1. Add the sliced kiwis, lime juice, baby spinach leaves, unsweetened coconut water, and chia seeds to a blender.

2. If you'd like, you can add sweetness by adding honey or maple syrup. The sweetness of the kiwis may be plenty.
3. Combine all the ingredients in a blender and process until you have a smooth, bright green smoothie.
4. You can blend the smoothie again after adding some ice cubes if you want it to be colder.
5. Taste the smoothie and adjust sweetness or consistency as per your preference.
6. Pour the Kiwi Lime Smoothie into two glasses.
7. Optional: Garnish with slices of kiwi and lime for a visually appealing touch.
8. Serve the refreshing and nutrient-packed Kiwi Lime Smoothie as a delightful and healthy breakfast or snack!

Nutritional Info Per Serving:

Calories: 80 | Fats: 2g | Carbs: 15g | Proteins: 2g | Potassium: 350mg | Sodium: 20mg

Almond Butter and Blueberry Smoothie

🕰 *Prep time: 5 minutes*

🍲 *Cook time: 0 minutes*

🍽 *Servings: 2*

🥤 **Ingredients:**

- 1 cup fresh or frozen blueberries
- 2 tablespoons almond butter
- 1 cup unsweetened almond milk (or any milk of your choice)
- 1 tablespoon chia seeds
- 1 tablespoon honey or maple syrup (optional, for added sweetness)
- 1/2 teaspoon vanilla extract
- Ice cubes (optional, if using fresh blueberries and you prefer a colder smoothie)

Directions:

1. Blend the almond butter, unsweetened almond milk, chia seeds, and vanilla extract in a blender with the blueberries.
2. If you'd like, you can add sweetness by adding honey or maple syrup. The sweetness of the blueberries themselves may be plenty.
3. Combine all the ingredients in a blender and process until you have a smooth, creamy purple smoothie.
4. You can blend the smoothie again after adding some ice cubes if you want it to be colder.
5. Taste the smoothie and adjust sweetness or consistency as per your preference.
6. Pour the Almond Butter and Blueberry Smoothie into two glasses.
7. Serve the antioxidant-rich and protein-packed Almond Butter and Blueberry Smoothie as a delicious and satisfying breakfast or snack!

Nutritional Info Per Serving:

Calories: 160 | Fats: 8g | Carbs: 20g | Proteins: 4g | Potassium: 200mg | Sodium: 85mg

Raspberry Avocado Smoothie

Prep time: 5 minutes
Cook time: 0 minutes
Servings: 2

Ingredients:

- 1 cup fresh or frozen raspberries
- 1 ripe avocado, peeled and pitted
- 1 cup unsweetened almond milk (or any milk of your choice)
- 1 tablespoon chia seeds
- 1 tablespoon honey or maple syrup (optional, for added sweetness)
- 1/2 teaspoon vanilla extract
- Ice cubes (optional, if using

fresh raspberries and you prefer a colder smoothie)

Directions:

1. Blend the raspberries, avocado that has reached peak ripeness, unsweetened almond milk, chia seeds, and vanilla extract in a blender.
2. If you'd like, you can add sweetness by adding honey or maple syrup. The natural sweetness of the raspberries and the smoothness of the avocado may be plenty.
3. Combine all the ingredients in a blender and process until you have a smooth, bright pink smoothie.
4. You can blend the smoothie again after adding some ice cubes if you want it to be colder.
5. Taste the smoothie and adjust sweetness or consistency to taste.
6. Pour the Raspberry Avocado Smoothie into two glasses.
7. Serve the antioxidant-rich and creamy Raspberry Avocado Smoothie as a delicious and nutritious breakfast or snack!

Nutritional Info Per Serving:

Calories: 200 | Fats: 12g | Carbs: 21g | Proteins: 4g | Potassium: 480mg | Sodium: 90mg

Green Goddess Smoothie

Prep time: 5 minutes
Cook time: 0 minutes
Servings: 2

Ingredients:

- 1 cup fresh spinach leaves
- 1 ripe avocado, peeled and pitted
- 1/2 cucumber, peeled and sliced
- 1 cup unsweetened coconut water (or any liquid of your choice)
- 1 tablespoon chia seeds
- 1 tablespoon honey or maple syrup (optional,

for added sweetness)
- Juice of 1/2 lemon
- Ice cubes (optional, for a colder smoothie)

⊠ Directions:

1. Add the fresh spinach leaves, ripe avocado, sliced cucumber, unsweetened coconut water, chia seeds, and lemon juice to a blender.
2. If you'd like, you can add sweetness by adding honey or maple syrup. Coconut water and the natural sweetness of the cucumber might be plenty.
3. Combine all the ingredients in a blender and process until you have a smooth, bright green smoothie.
4. You can blend the smoothie again after adding some ice cubes if you want it to be colder.
5. Taste the smoothie and adjust sweetness or consistency to taste.
6. Pour the Green Goddess Smoothie into two glasses.
7. Serve the nutrient-packed and refreshing Green Goddess Smoothie as a delicious and energizing breakfast or snack!

Nutritional Info Per Serving:
Calories: 220 | Fats: 15g | Carbs: 21g | Proteins: 5g | Potassium: 760mg | Sodium: 50mg

Measurement Conversion Chart

Volume Equivalents (Liquid)

US STANDARD	US STANDARD (OZ.)	METRIC (APPROXIMATE)
2 tbsp.	1 fl. oz.	30 mL
¼ cup	2 fl. oz.	60 mL
1/2 cup	4 fl. oz.	120 mL
1 cup	8 fl. oz.	240 mL
11/2 cups	12 fl. oz.	355 mL
2 cups or 1 pint	16 fl. oz.	475 mL
4 cups or 1 quart	32 fl. oz.	1 L
1 gallon	128 fl. oz.	4 L

Volume Equivalents (Dry)

US STANDARD	METRIC (APPROXIMATE)
¼ tsp.	1 mL
½ tsp.	2 mL
1 tsp.	5 mL
1 tbsp.	15 mL
¼ cup	59 mL
1/3 cup	79 mL
1/2 cup	118 mL
1 cup	177 mL

US STANDARD	METRIC (APPROXIMATE)
1/2 oz.	15 g
1 oz.	30 g
2 oz.	60 g
4 oz.	115 g
8 oz.	225 g
12 oz.	340 g
16 oz. or 1 pound	455 g

Index

Printed in Great Britain
by Amazon

38029131R00056